Press Gang

Press Gang

Roy Hattersley

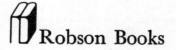 Robson Books

The author and publishers would like to thank the editor
and proprietors of *Punch* magazine (and the editor of the
Guardian) for their kind permission to reproduce material
first published in their pages.

FIRST PUBLISHED IN GREAT BRITAIN BY ROBSON
BOOKS LTD., BOLSOVER HOUSE, 5–6 CLIPSTONE
STREET, LONDON W1P 7EB. COPYRIGHT © 1983
ROY HATTERSLEY

British Library Cataloguing in Publication Data

Hattersley, Roy
   Press gang.
   I. Title
   082   PR6058.A/

   ISBN 0–86051–212–6

Phototypesetting by Strewlight Ltd., London W1P 7EB

Printed in Great Britain by Biddles Ltd., Guildford

Contents

Introduction

I was well into my teens before I understood that newspapers were supposed to do something more than record football results, report cricket matches and repeat long passages from Parliamentary speeches. I vaguely realized that there was a hierarchy of both newspapers and newspaper readers and that I was expected to feel pity for people who bought the *Sheffield Star* to read 'births marriages and deaths', and contempt for the families who spent their day of rest with the *News of the World*. But I was fourteen (I remember the date because my exact contemporary Albert Quixall was in his last year with Sheffield Schoolboys) when I first understood that the better dailies amused as well as informed, and the worst were as biased as they were boring. Ever since then I have been something between intrigued and obsessed with the vast divide separating the best and the worst in British journalism.

During the last two years the weekly *Press Gang* which I have written for *Punch* has, alas, dealt more with Fleet Street's failings than with its triumphs — though *Punch* and I have managed to give some credit where credit was obviously due. The encomium to the *Daily Express* for its 'Intruder in the Palace' story was written into that newspaper's citation when it won Granada Television's 'Scoop of the Year Award'. Proper homage was paid to Posy Simmonds's *Guardian* cartoon in a column which is included in this anthology slightly incongruously in the 'Court and Social' section for no better reason than the necessity to celebrate the Weber family somewhere. Though I accept that they are unlikely to appear either at a Buckingham Palace investiture or at the altar in St Margaret's, Westminster.

In between those two articles *Press Gang* examined the quality of newspapers writing against the definition of journalism laid down by T.S. Eliot — the 'type of mind . . . which can only turn to writing or produce its best writing under the pressure of an immediate occasion.' When I first heard that description I thought, at once, of 'Old International' in the *Manchester Guardian* tapping out his football reports. 'If Derek Dooley is a dunce,' he announced after that phenomenal centre forward had scored two goals against Burnley in a mid-week match, 'the Burnley supporters would like their team to have eleven such dunces on the books.' It was the *Guardian* sports writers who taught me that elegance and excitement can go together. I still marvel at the good fortune or judgement that has given one paper Neville Cardus, John Arlott and Frank Keating in succession.

In their time they have all had to obey the Eliot Rule and write at speed after close of play. The habits of Alan Watkins, Simon Hoggart, David McKie, Fiona McDonald-Hull and Keith Waterhouse are unknown to me. But *Press Gang* was pleased to pay humble and envious tribute to the quality of writing that each of those dissimilar journalists produced. As if to prove my complimentary point, I mis-spelled Miss McDonald-Hull's name. That error, and similar foolish mistakes, has been corrected here. Apart from the eradication of absurdities, each piece appears as it was originally published in *Punch*. (Those curious to know when that was should turn to pages 191-192.)

They have been arranged in eight sections, each containing seven articles. 'Court and Social' concerns Fleet Street's strange relationship with the Royal Family and its abiding interest in matters of class and convention. For seven of the first twenty months of *Press Gang's* life, the Falkland Islands were in the news every day. 'Down Argentina Way' deals with how the newspapers treated the crisis — and how the Government treated the newspapers' treatment. 'Within the Fringe' describes the publications — ranging from *Militant* to the *Jewish Chronicle* — which are part of the penumbra of the Press. Some of them are weekly publications. But the better-known magazines have a section all to themselves —

8

'Once a Week'. It pays respect to several 'lovely reads'.

Inevitably 'Private Grief' and 'Only on Sundays' overlap. For 'Private Grief' deals with prurience, and the *News of the World* comes out on Sundays. Since that medium and that message are inseparable, the 'Exclusive Confession of Doctor Death's Mistress' could have appeared under either heading. So could the account of Malcolm Muggeridge's christening which appeared in so many Sunday papers. It appears in 'Private Grief' even though the subject of the story encouraged reporters to peer through the keyhole of the Catholic Church at a ceremony which should not have attracted the full public relations treatment.

The section on politics ('Lobby Terms') and the collection of pieces on proprietors ('Nine-Tenths of the Law') are equally movable — though whether or not they are feasts is more open to doubt. The refusal of Trafalgar House (which owns both the *Daily Express* and the *Cunard Company*) to allow patriotism to stand in the way of profit might have appeared under the Falklands flag. 'The Honest Man' is the single article in this collection which was not published in *Punch*. It was originally intended for *Press Gang*. But I subsequently decided that it was more suitable for the *Guardian*. I was wrong. It has now returned to its natural home.

The pieces on proprietors combine with those on intrusion into private life to represent a growing anxiety about the behaviour of our national newspapers. The ideological prejudice of the British Press is a fact of political life. It is spuriously described by the beneficiaries of the bias as the inevitable outcome of a free society. And supporters of the party which is so bitterly opposed by six-and-a-half of Fleet Street's nine national publications regard the antics of the *Daily Mail* and *Sun* as one of the hazards of their existence, for which they must make plans in the way that they prepare for snow and the late arrival of railway trains.

But other aspects of the Fourth Estate's behaviour cause increasing anxiety to philosophical friends and political foes in almost equal measure. Chequebook in hand, foot in door, kneeling for the accolade of knighthood to brush the shoulder — every posture causes some sort of concern. It is for that reason that I have taken as my epilogue a preview of the House of Commons debate on a Bill to provide the statutory right of reply. It took place two weeks after the Press Council's condemnation of the way in which the *Daily Mail*, amongst other papers, had treated the 'Yorkshire Ripper' story, and two weeks less one day after the editor of that up-market tabloid published his rejection of the Press Council's findings.

Every speech in that debate was a sort of warning. Some called for immediate legislation. Others hoped that self-improvement would make official remedies unnecessary. No one was satisfied with behaviour that ranged from inventing interviews to buying witnesses' memoirs. In my view, too few of the Honourable and Right Honourable Members prefaced their criticisms with comments about the better side of Fleet Street and the premises that house the magazines. For in the *Economist* and the *Observer*, the *Guardian* and *The Listener*, the *Mirror* and the *Financial Times* (not to mention *Punch*), Britain possesses publications for which any journalist should feel privileged to work. I doubt if *Press Gang* maintains a proper balance between the excellent and the execrable. But then, as it is in itself part of British journalism, it is hardly likely to be perfect.

R.H.

Down Argentina Way

By Jingo!

THE INDICTMENT CAN be clearly stated. The Argentine invasion of the Falkland Isles took them by complete surprise. After initially perceiving the danger, they allowed their attention to be diverted by politically more attractive — but nationally less vital — issues. In failure they are all the more fatuous because of their traditional posture as protectors of what is left of the Empire and supporters of what remains of the imperial armed forces. Now, the danger is that they will look at the South Atlantic in terms of their own reputation rather than the realities of our military strength and the needs of the Falklanders. It was a bad ten days for the *Daily Express* and its Sunday sister paper.

Forty-eight hours before the first Argentine Marine landed at Port Stanley the *Daily Express* led with 'Falkland Fiasco'. Political editor John Warden reported that 'submarines of the Royal Navy are to patrol the Falkland Islands . . . in case diplomacy fails to repulse the Argentine threat.' But that was not the fiasco to which the headline referred. Chief reporter Michael Brown revealed that the Argentine 'invasion force were scrap-metal Steptoes with not a soldier in sight' and that they invited the British explorers 'who pounced on them' to dinner. 'What happens now?' the *Express* asked. 'Does our gunboat the *Endurance* . . . land Marines to turf the Argies off?'

The following day, whilst the Argies' own Marines were steaming towards the Falklands, the *Express* changed its front page tack. 'It's so much BETTER for Maggie' the banner headlines screamed. The story (based on a Mori opinion pole) justified the joy — 'Voters are swinging back to

13

the Tories and things look good for Maggie.' The Falkland Islands rated sixty-six words on page two. The 'Opinion' column was headed 'Dreams, jobs and reality'. It concluded that the country was 'beginning to turn back to the Government.'

On the fatal Friday the *Daily Express* had an inside column 'Falkland Invasion "Imminent" '. But the quotation marks that surrounded the final word were a clear indication that the idea of an imminent landing was not a notion that the *Express* endorsed. It was in fact the judgement of Sir Anthony Parsons, Britain's Ambassador at the United Nations. If the *Express* had accepted his opinion it would no doubt have put the story in a more prominent place. The front page proclaimed that war had broken out — but only in the SDP. The 'Opinion' column demanded conscription — but for 'community care, conservation and domestic peace'.

The following day, when news of the Argentine landing had reached both Fleet Street and the Foreign Office, the *Daily Express* unfurled its battle ensign. 'Invasion of the Falkland Islands' occupied the whole front page. A picture claiming to embrace all the 1,813 inhabitants was sandwiched between a description of their status and our duty. 'Our loyal subjects — we MUST defend them.' Inside the paper five whole pages (each one decorated by a picture of the plumed-hatted Governor), were devoted to the beleaguered British outpost. Lord Carrington was excoriated for incompetence. The Ministry of Defence was castigated for being ill-prepared. Apparently they realized the danger too late.

The *Sunday Express* announced that 'Heads will roll' but retained its dog-like devotion to the Prime Minister who, it said, 'yesterday proclaimed Britain's sense of outrage and the need for action'. Lord George-Brown was wheeled in to call for calm. The editor, Sir John Junor, either did not read the article or did not heed it. His leader used all the catch-phrases — 'blunder' — 'fiasco' — 'humiliation'. In his 'Current Events' column he put the personal boot in with his usual bovver-boy relish. 'As for our pathetic Defence Secretary, did it never occur to him that the thirteen British frigates which have for the last two weeks been buzzing around in the Mediterranean would have been better employed buzzing around South Georgia?' Perhaps Mr Nott became complacent

14

by reading the *Daily Express.*

If Mr Nott is an *Express* reader he cannot have enjoyed the April 5th edition. On page two he was named as one of 'Mrs Thatcher's guilty men'. Once upon a time, naming guilty men (usually procurers, ponces and pimps) was a regular preoccupation of fearless fighting papers. In those good old days the slightly up-market *Daily Express* eschewed vice and corruption and ran personal vendettas against politicians who did not take Lord Beaverbrook's fancy. Most of the *Express* campaigns flopped and its victims became Prime Minister of India or Chief of the Defence Staff. But last week one of the victims was actually victimized. 'Blame' said the *Express* under a picture of Lord Carrington. The following day he resigned.

Next to the picture of the luckless Lord were little reproductions of two earlier *Express* front pages — giving the impression that the paper had been pounding on about the Falkland Islands for days. On Tuesday April 6th it pounded away with a vengeance, producing a cover feature of the Prime Minister and Lord Carrington under the heading 'leader and loser'. Mrs Thatcher — as if to emphasize her martial mood — was shown wearing the sort of little black fur hat *de rigeur* amongst light infantry drummer boys in the late nineteenth century. To ram the message home, John Warden added a helpful note at the bottom of a column which proclaimed that Mrs Thatcher had 'taken firm command of the crisis'. She had, he explained, paraphrased Queen Victoria who said 'we are not interested in the politics of defeat'.

The rest was all ships and sea — making fastidious *Express* readers (if such people exist) grateful that their paper had chosen to compare Mrs Thatcher with Queen Victoria rather than Elizabeth 1 addressing the fleet at Tilbury. But patriotism was not the predominant theme. 'Opinion' ended with a paragraph that printed 'affrontery' on every jingoistic column:

> 'God's in his heaven; all's right with the world; Mrs Thatcher must have been thinking, until suddenly her world crashed around her. The pound tumbles, £2,000 million is wiped off share values and apprehension fills

the air. Tough luck? Not really. Poor judgement.'

Exactly.

Picture Search

JOURNALISM IS THE most cynical of all the professions and politics is the most naive. But when the lives of writers and speakers overlap, both eye each other with the same wary suspicion. Politicians believe that journalists are never to be trusted. And they are *wrong*. Journalists believe that most politicians try to manipulate them. And they are right. When the relationship is further complicated by the intervention of civil servants who despise both trades, the result is chaos of connoisseur quality. That is, more or less, what happened over the planning and execution of the information war in the South Atlantic. Thus Britain lost most of the early battles.

In Fleet Street, Broadcasting House and the modest Wells Street headquarters of Independent Television News the suspicion that the Government manipulates the news always bubbles beneath the smooth surface of proper respect for Ministers. Even the papers that support the party in power are careful not to be denied information which the Administration thinks best kept under lock and key in Whitehall. In general, such self-defensive vigilance is justified. Governments do try to manage tomorrow's front page and tonight's news bulletin. But fears about the intentional suppression of news from the Falkland Islands and their dependencies were probably unfounded. The failure to provide facilities for television pictures was a tragedy, but not a conspiracy.

At first there almost certainly was a desperate fear in the Ministry of Defence that our military effort could be undermined by pictures of the battles to recapture sovereign British territory being brought into our living rooms each night and on to our breakfast tables each morning. The war in Vietnam was largely lost on the monitors of CBS and NBC. And America's unhappy experience must have argued caution when the Task Force set sail south. If the Ministry of

16

Defence was not being intentionally obstructive, then its officials acted with an unthinking obstinacy which more imaginative men will find hard to comprehend. The likelihood is that the second explanation — incompetence not conspiracy — is correct.

You will recall that the Argentine invasion of the Falkland Islands came as something of a surprise to the Foreign Office, and that General Galtieri discovered that once the message reached the MoD the Task Force was assembled with hitherto inconceivable speed. Both the aggression and the response caught the Government Information Service off guard. Leslie Jeans, the head of public relations at Defence, retired in 1981. His successor was to take over this week [16 June 1982].

In the meantime, Ian McDonald was to be in charge. Mr McDonald no doubt possesses many admirable qualities. But he is not, and never has been, a journalist. Defence Ministry information officers who have never held a NUJ card often go far. One has become Private Secretary to the Queen. But they worry professional journalists.

Concern was increased when on April 13th, the new head of public relations, Neville Taylor, late of the Environment Department, took up his post three months ahead of schedule. Within days of his arrival he was handed a note from Sir Frnk Cooper, the Permanent Under-Secretary. It told him that McDonald would remain in charge of matters concerning the South Atlantic. The instruction has now been either withdrawn or countermanded. But the idea of a conspiracy gained ground. The refusal to help with the transmission of pictures by installing a satellite ground station, either aboard a Task Force ship or on the San Carlos beach-head, began to look like wilful obstruction.

The Ministry of Defence claim that the spirit was willing but the technology weak. A station lashed amidships of one of Her Majesty's capital ships would only have worked if the man-o'-war had been stationed so far away from the early action that it played no part in the actual military operation. Whilst the BBC claims that a satellite could be fed from San Carlos 'in the time that it takes to make the decision and fly it down there' in a single Hercules transport, the MoD say that the best prospect is a portable transmitter in Mexico 'the size

17

of three Portakabins'. To fly it to the Task Force, the Government would need three Hercules and a quick answer about who would pay the million pound bill for purchase and installation.

While technical arguments about the need for a 'stable aerial' and the possible use of a military satellite continue, there is general agreement that the failure to produce up-to-date television film has 'made it more difficult to carry world opinion'. That was the opinion of the Minstry of Defence the day after the bombing of the troop landing-craft at Port Stanley. At the same time, they were still insisting that they were waiting for the BBC to 'provide advice on equipment'. Everyone agrees that, 'with hindsight', provision should have been made for television pictures. The hope now is that Britain's reputation for honest reporting will overcome the disadvantage of being weeks behind the Argentine in the transmission war.

In the war of words, the relationship between the Ministry of Defence and the broadcasters is almost ideal. All 'voice traffic' from the South Atlantic is fed into the BBC where the recording equipment is permanently manned. The MoD 'listen across the line' to the correspondent filing his despatch. If they hear information which might, when broadcast, put the Task Force at risk, a 'request' for silence is justified with the facts of the military case. Both parties agree that the scheme has worked well. Only once has a broadcast gone ahead against Ministry advice. The BBC refused to wait whilst the civil servants made up their minds about the dangers of one story. When they came to a final conclusion, they approved the transmission.

But the battles over television equipment rage on. The BBC claims that it has never heard of the Mexican connection and that spending a million pounds on buying a Central American major station would be absurd when ITN has a portable unit ready for shipment. Meanwhile Brian Hanrahan and Michael Nicholson are thrown back on the report's greatest asset and last refuge — words. No one can doubt that they are producing graphic acounts of the courage and the suffering that make up the Falklands war. But the public are entitled to see as well as hear what is being done in their name.

18

Paper Tigers

THERE HAVE BEEN times during the last week or two when I began to suspect that the Soviet Union had entered the war in the South Atlantic on the side of Argentina and was assisting its recently acquired allies by sprinkling Fleet Street with some terrible item from the arsenal of germ warfare that softened the brains of tabloid journalists. The *Sun's* sustained xenophobic hysteria has become the most notorious example of marble loss. But whilst that paper has certainly preserved a high idiocy quotient more consistently than any of its rivals, the *Daily Mail* managed in one issue to rise to the heights of lunacy which no other paper was able to match.

Faithful as always to Mrs Thatcher, the *Mail* responded to her criticism of the way that radio and television are reporting the crisis by allowing Andrew Alexander (normally a Parliamentary sketchwriter) to spread himself across the leader page with a thousand-word fantasy. I know Mr Alexander to be invariably prejudiced, often offensive, and occasionally inaccurate. But the idea that he is a mystic or medium of the sort much in demand at spiritualist meetings and seances had never before struck me. However, in the *Daily Mail* he recounted, verbatim, a recent interview on the Falklands crisis, given by Sir Winston Churchill.

Sir Winston was cross-examined, presumably from the big studio in the sky, by three anonymous, but pusillanimous, inquisitors who share all of the shortcomings of their craven profession. A drawing of the unique event decorated the top of the exclusive page. Churchill looked like the Sutherland portrait after cosmetic surgery. The journalists were suitably shadowy figures — the sort of men who appease aggression, care little for national honour and undermine the war effort for appearance money. They were also appalling interviewers.

For they managed to elicit nothing new or original from their distinguished guest. He actually replied to one of their questions with the offer of nothing except 'blood, sweat, toil and tears'. One of them allowed himself to become diverted into an irrelevance about why Sir Winston pronounces 'Nazi' in such an idiosyncratic fashion. If such an interview had *really* taken place it would not have been worth publishing. The invention of such a farrago is awful proof of how parts of Fleet Street sank all sense of proportion in the South Atlantic.

The *Daily Mail* was not, of course, alone. The *Sun's* behaviour was consistently deplorable in almost every way. One of their issues actually boasted about the paper 'sponsoring' a missile — a story that shows either an unparalleled ignorance or a callous disregard for human life that beggars description. Presumably, the *Sun's* executives know that missiles are intended to kill people. Deaths in the South Atlantic may be both unavoidable and justified. My objection to the *Sun's* attitude is similar to the proper complaint about fox-hunting. Sinking Argentine ships may be necessary, but enjoying it is morally indefensible.

A little hyperbole was, of course, to be expected. The Prime Minister entered the crisis as the reincarnation of Queen Victoria when she refused to contemplate defeat. Later, there was a touch of the Boadicea. No doubt the *Sun* thought it had scooped the extravagant-image pool with the suggestion that Mrs Thatcher was 'Britannia come to life'. But it may well be that the *Mail on Sunday* won the jackpot of excess in the end. Peter Simmonds, the political editor, found her 'resolve to drive out the Argentines' reminiscent of General Douglas MacArthur in the Philippines. We can only presume that Mr Simmonds, not having read any of the biographies about the General's vainglorious obsession with contrived glory, meant to be complimentary.

The *Sun's* intention in attacking everyone and anyone whom it regarded as less than passionate in the patriotic cause, appeared, at first read, to be more the result of idiocy than ignorance. After closer inspection, its motives seemed more complex. It attached Peter Snow of the BBC, Les Gibbard (cartoonist) of the *Guardian* and, above all, the leader writers of the *Mirror*. The charge against all of them was treason. The *Mirror* was said to support 'appeasing the Argentine dictator' and trading 'peace for honour'; charges that confirm the view that, whatever their intellectual shortcomings, the people who run the *Sun* can at least read and understand the opinion polls.

The surveys proclaim that the popular paper buying

public is passionately in favour of teaching the Argies a lesson. And the people who buy the *Sun* are, on the evidence, at the forefront of the call for swift and decisive military action. William Randolph Hearst founded part of his American newspaper empire on events further north in the Americas. He sold papers by whipping up anti-Cuban fervour. Horatio Bottomley pushed up *John Bull's* circulation by fomenting war fever. Northcliffe helped the *Mail* to survive into the twentieth century by demanding no mercy for the Boers. I say it with the greatest regret. But I suspect that the cartoon of General Galtieri decorated with a medal designed in the form of a death-laden destroyer did no harm to circulation.

Not that I believe the *Sun's* decision to follow the path of paranoid patriotism was wholly cynical. I suspect that the vulgarians who run that paper get real enjoyment out of the headlines like 'Stick that up your Junta' and perhaps even convince themselves that they are serving some patriotic cause as well as increasing Mr Rupert Murdoch's income.

But, of course, their respect for the flag and admiration for our 'crack shots' who 'scared the Argies' does not stand in the way of their publishing one of the nasty little stories for which the paper is famous. On the day that the *Sun's* leader praised 'our men' who knew 'that the price of freedom might have to be paid in blood' yet 'never flinched', page five led with a story of the 'wife of Marine hero in shoplifting probe'. The lady in question was not charged by the police. But the 'shoplifting allegations' were all reported alongside her photograph and that of her husband who had taken part in the recapture of South Georgia. In the *Sun's* own words, such behaviour in Buenos Aires would result in the offending journalist being shot. In Britain, it only excites contempt.

Articles of War

ACCORDING TO THE *Sunday Times*, the Ministry of Defence went on to the attack last week [8 September 1982]. 'Tired of the accusation that it had obstructed coverage of the

Falklands Conflict,' the story ran, 'the MoD has decided to answer back' and confront its critics face to face.

The organizers of the Edinburgh Television Festival who had promoted the event and were acting as matchmakers were anxious to explain that they, for their part, did not regard the contest as an opportunity for acrimonious recrimination. Indeed, what was called 'tit-for-tat' was specifically ruled out. The late afternoon in Edinburgh was to be spent in a constructive attempt to agree on how the frictions and frustrations could be avoided if ever we had to send a Task Force anywhere again.

To start us off, Admiral 'Teddy' Whetstone, Assistant Chief of Naval Staff (Operations), and Neville Taylor, Head of Public Relations at the Ministry of Defence, would explain the problems of getting news home from distant, beleaguered islands. David Nicholas, Editor of ITN, and Peter Woon, Head of BBC News, would then help us all to learn the lessons of the South Atlantic.

It was to be a highly civilized affair. And so it initially turned out to be. For the first half hour, neither side laid a glove on each other. I suspect that some members of the packed audience expected — and looked forward to — a good punch-up. But Paul Fox, the Managing Director of Yorkshire Television, who refereed the contest, was not the sort of official who calls reluctant fighter together and warns them that if they do not give the customers value for money he will cancel the contest and revoke their licences. Mr Fox did, however, describe the dilemma that ought to have dominated the subsequent discussion.

The same manual which was issued to journalists who went to Suez was handed out to the reporters sailing to the South Atlantic twenty-five years later. 'The essence of successful warfare,' it asserted, 'is secrecy. The essence of successful journalism is publication.'

The conflict of two equally legitimate but mutually contradictory interests should have dominated the two hours of discussion which followed. And Messrs Nicholas and Woon did make mild and gentlemanly attempts to expose some real issues ' . . . some censorship accepted on common-sense grounds . . . the spectre of Vietnam and the anti-war effect of TV pictures of burnt villages and dying marines . . . everyone

22

surprised by the national mood . . . '

But there were too many old media soldiers in the audience who wanted to re-live The Battle of Lime Grove. The Landing on *Panorama*, The Assault on *TV Eye* and the long campaign against MoD information officers. It turned out to be an afternoon of war (of words) memoirs.

With the exception, that is, of the two men who had really been at the Front (Brian Hanrahan and Michael Nicholson) and Admiral Whetstone. I am by no means certain that ACNS (Ops) made his increasingly significant contribution on purpose. For he had begun by saying that his prominent place on the platform had come as a surprise to him — a shock which we must in part attribute to his failure to read the *Sunday Times*, where his performance was previewed. But having started by listing the Navy's undisputed and indisputable 'Guidelines for Releasing News to the Press' (News must be true. Lives must not be put at risk. Next-of-kin must be protected) he increasingly revealed the real concerns of 'Them' who must decide what is good for 'Us'.

Admiral Whetstone made the disarming admission that for some military men, 'The ideal war is the one in which the troops come back first and are followed by the report that they have won.' But whilst he dismissed such primitive nonsence, he did urge us to accept other realities. 'Back at home there were political issues to be considered — not the defence of a particular Government — but a defence of our position in world opinion.' And the MoD had understood completely that whilst during the last war 'the conflict between patriotic duty and the duty to report information' had always been resolved in the national interest, times had changed. 'The duty to report information has been regarded as increasingly important over recent years.'

It was, of course, not the only item of interest. Mr Hanrahan and Mr Nicholson were as impressive in their descriptions of 'neither conspiracy, nor cock-up, but inertia' and the proper balance between 'the sensible and the necessary and the absurd' as they were in their accounts of Bluff Cove and Tumbledown Mountain. And that is very impressive indeed.

Mr Alan Clarke, MP, gave his now celebrated imitation of a Dickensian villain, sitting on the edge of a table swinging his two-tone shoes and denouncing a *Panorama* programme as 'teeth-gnashingly odious' — a description he defended even when he was eventually convinced that the interview to which he objected appeared in *TV Eye*.

But then somebody raised the question about the effect on public opinion of screening pictures of death and mutilation — children burning with napalm in South-East Asia, old ladies sitting amongst the Beirut ruins, soldiers being executed by their own officers, prisoners being beaten until they described the disposition of the regiments from which they had deserted.

The servicemen present could not have been more frank. Of course the sight of war, in all its brutal reality, would sap the national will to fight. Was it, they asked, in the national interest to have our national morale undermined by a free press, whilst the totalitarians kept their scenes of death and destruction off the breakfast table? They were only asking.

I offer only one clue to the answer they might give. Alan Percival, a young MoD information officer who had actually been in the Falklands, rose to defend his Department. The moment that white flags were sighted in Port Stanley, he said, helicopters were provided to fly the newsmen to the scene of the surrender. I never doubted it. But it did convince me that truth is far too important to be left to the generals.

Foreign Matter

MOST OF LAST week's *News of the World* was a connoisseur's issue. In the north, General Sir Jeremy Moore led the front page with mildly indiscreet comments about joining 'Britain's army of unemployed'. But in the later, southern editions, the human interest exclusive about 'the commander who fought the Falklands war with a Bible in his knapsack' was pushed literally aside. The Prime Minister in Port Stanley is the stuff that banner headlines are made of. So, like every other Sunday paper, the *News of the World* changed its lead to accommodate 'Maggie in Falklands'. But the rest of the paper was like a satire of Saturday night in Bouverie Street.

Private Eye could not hope to invent headlines of such prurient triviality as 'Carnal beast's victim relives night of hell' or 'Kidney op may make Eddie a dad'. And 'Horror of cats killed by witches' has, like 'Vicar hits our at "evil matron"', a distinctive charm which marks it out as an extract from Britain's Biggest Selling Newspaper. The story in which 'Top TV grappler, Adrian Street' revealed 'the ugly truth' about 'corruption and vice' in all-in wrestling was a sick joke. And what 'Sexy showgirl Suzy Silver' had to say about 'the secret passion in the life of tragic comedy star Dick Emery' was just sick.

But one sentence on the leader page did not have the *News of the World* health warning stamped so prominently upon it. Indeed it appeared, in almost identical form in the *Sunday Times* of the same day. Both papers told us that when Francis Pym, the Foreign Secretary, won the Military Cross, part of the citation for it read 'he carried on as if nothing had happened'. I do not believe that Paul Potts — despite the enormous improvement he has made in *News of the World* political coverage — was actually shown the citation by Mr Pym. Indeed, I suspect that the reticent Francis, being an ex-officer and a current gentleman, was deeply embarrassed by the publication of what the code of honour requires to be kept private. Yet the same quotation appeared twice on the same Sunday. I blame neither misfortune nor carelessness, but the Foreign Office.

For the Foreign Office talks to newspapers collectively and individually, covertly and blatantly, dispassionately and obsessively, all the time and in every possible way. In only one other Department of State do the Civil Servants so regularly brief the Press and get away with it. And even in the Treasury, there is usually a *frisson* of embarrassment when some national daily announces that, in the mandarins' collegiate view, the Chancellor or the Prime Minister is wrong. When that happens in the field of Foreign Policy there is much rejoicing on the more fashionable side of Downing Street. The FCO feels publicly absolved from responsibility for current folies. And in clubs and senior common-rooms all over the civilized world, men of judgement are heartened by renewed proof that at least 'the Office' has kept its head when all about it etc, etc.

I promise you that during the desperate days that lie ahead — the discussion of the Franks Report on the causes of the Falklands invasion and the current conflict between Foreign Secretary and Prime Minister — the FCO will win the war of words in the serious papers. They may be excoriated in the *Sun*, denounced in the *Daily Mail* and ridiculed in the *Express*. But they will triumph in the *The Times*, the *Daily Telegraph* and the *Guardian*. The editorials may be critical. But the news stories (which are really what form opinion) will bear the mark of 'the Office'. There are three reasons which justify a modest gamble on its success.

First, 'the Office' — like the Treasury — boasts an independent identity that transcends the opinions of individual governments and outlasts the brief prejudices of single Ministers. There is a Foreign Office view on the world, which may or may not coincide with that of the Administration which it serves.

Consider the causes of our present discontents. Do you know the Department of Employment view on 3,000,000 unemployed? Or the Ministry of Agriculture's opinion of the Common Agricultural Policy? Or the Home Office's position on immigration control?

In other departments we know what the Minister thinks, not the Ministry. 'The Foreign Office advise . . . ' wrote the *News of the World*. 'Pym', the *Sunday Times* explained, ' . . . followed the long-held FO line.' Neither paper would write of the Department of the Environment as if it existed independently of its Secretary of State.

Secondly, the Foreign Office always employs one of its own official spokesmen. Sometimes the Treasury does the same. It occasionally appoints a volunteer from its administrative ranks to justify the ways of God to men. Or — as in the case of Peter Middleton, the next Permanent Secretary — a civil servant of unusual talent is switched backwards and forwards between 'information' and 'policy'. But in the rest of the domestic departments a special caste called 'information officers' disseminates Ministry news. Sometimes they develop an inconvenient loyalty to ministers and the government of which those ministers are a part.

In the FO, they do things differently. The 'Head of News Department' is a proper diplomat — or always has been except for the one occasion when Jim Callaghan brought in an outsider. He identifies with 'the Office' and expects to rise within it. And perhaps more important, although he speaks for the Diplomatic Service, he is not a lone voice. Nobody who has ever eaten lunch at the Reform Club doubts that the Treasury talks to journalists. But they do not 'brief' and 'advise' with the same single-mindedness as the men who did it out of duty in Washington and Paris, and go on doing it out of conviction in London.

So when you read the stories on the Franks Report, remember that the Foreign Office has a special way with newspapers. And remember too the third ingrained advantage. It is usually right.

Less Than Franks

ALL CREDIT TO the *Observer*. Forty-eight hours before official publication, its banner headline was confident and categoric about the Falkland Isles report. 'Franks finds Thatcher is not to blame', was splashed across its front page over an 'exclusive' story. The author — Adam Raphael — insists that there was no leak. He neither saw the document on which he commented nor had its contents been tittle-tattled. He simply used his initiative and judgement, pursuing not the six wise men on the committee but the inumerable witnesses who provided their evidence. In short, Mr Raphael claims that he constructed a parallel report and drew the intelligent conclusion. Who are we to argue with him?

It is Mr Raphael's success in holding a Franks inquiry of his own and gaining from it an accurate assessment of the real report's conclusions that makes the behaviour of Bernard Ingham so difficult to understand. Mr Ingham is the Prime Minister's Press Secretary. So he saw the results of the Falklands investigation as soon as they were submitted to Mrs Thatcher. He knew that the final paragraph concluded that no one would 'be justified in attaching any criticism to the present Government', and he must have therefore expected the Press to do their patriotic duty — i.e. idolatrize the Prime Minister. Yet he behaved in a way which opened him to the charge of attempted manipulation.

I describe his behaviour in that neutral way for three reasons. One: In the circumstances, manipulation was unnecessary. With the recently knighted David English in command and the material which the report provided, no power on earth could have prevented the *Daily Mail* splashing, 'Not Guilty. First to raise the alert was Maggie.' Two: Mr Ingham asssured me that all he tried to do was help journalists 'find their way around' Franks. Three: He gave me that assurance in such belicose language that failure to report his disclaimer would put my person at risk when next I meet the burly Mr Ingham.

Nevertheless his conduct on the day of the report's publication was at best naive and the explanations which followed were (to be charitable) disingenuous. The facts can be clearly stated. The Franks Report (all 109 pages) was made available to Press, public and Parliament only at 3.30 p.m. on the afternoon of Tuesday, 18th January at the exact moment when Mrs Thatcher began to make her statement on its contents. Mr Ingham, conscious of the problems which this would cause for journalists, offered help.

He suggested that at 2.45 he addressed a meeting of 'the Lobby' — that elite band of Parliamentary Correspondents which never betrays a confidence. He was prepared, three-quarters of an hour before they actually saw the report, 'to point out the important paragraphs' in a document which (at least according to its authors) ought to be considered as a whole. Unfortunately, some of the political journalists who might have benefited from his guidance made his offer public. The Prime Minister was so incensed by the implied slur on the integrity of her faithful servant that she forbade him to go on with the proposed spoon-feeding. The ingrates had to fend for themselves. And they managed their lonely obligation very well.

None better than John Warden, the Political Editor of the *Daily Express*. Mr Warden is this year's chairman of 'the Lobby'. Because he holds that office, he went with Mrs

Thatcher on her tour of the liberated islands. And in that capacity he upbraided his indiscreet colleagues for biting the hand with which Bernard Ingham proposed to feed them a pre-digested version of the Franks Report. But surely, he did himself, and his colleagues, less than justice. With or without Mr Ingham's help, 'The Voice of Britain' would have celebrated: 'Mrs Thatcher scored another Falklands victory last night by yomping all over the fiercest critics.'

The *Daily Telegraph* was only slightly less predictable. 'Thatcher is Exonerated' probably wins the year's award for the longest word to appear in a banner headline. But there was nothing else of novelty in the paper. Godfrey Barker — now firmly entrenched in the pretentious tradition of *Telegraph* sketch writers — made a singularly inapposite comparison between the Danish Court receiving news of Ophelia's death and the Opposition in the House of Commons listening to the Prime Minister's statement. And its leader writers acknowledged the importance of the subject not by the profundity of their judgements but by the length down the page of their ponderous editorial.

But as compared with the comment column in the *Daily Mail*, the *Telegraph* editorial was a model of moderation. The *Mail* produced a passage of prose which was clearly intended to be purple, but came out in the wash as a slightly streaky mauve. 'The slate has been wiped clean. Britain under Mrs Thatcher did win a glorious victory for freedom. Now let there be an end to the carping.' What carping did they have in mind? Perhaps they were pertubed by a paragraph six inches higher on the same page. 'Lord Carrington wishes he had sent a submarine on March 5th . . . but he didn't.' Or are we allowed to go on carping at the Foreign Office and the Tory wets as long as we acknowledge Mrs Thatcher's 'glorious victory'?

Compared with all this, *The Times* ('Thatcher cleared of Falklands blame by Franks') and the *Guardian* ('Thatcher is cleared of Falklands blame') seem like paragons of calm objectivity and balance — even though they could not manage an apostrophe between them. *The Times* even found room to report the one policy point that came out of the report's publication — "Fortress Falklands seen as only option". And the *Financial Times* managed to produce

'Franks says Government not to blame for Junta's invasion.' These three papers, I suspect, enjoyed the services of journalists who read the report for themselves, rather than relying on Bernard Ingham's assistance.

For despite the Prime Minister's stern injunction, Mr Ingham did come to the aid of the bewildered Press. Of course, he did not brief them before they saw the report. But after Mrs Thatcher's House of Commons statement, some lost souls did ask him 'to give them a quick run-through'. That is how Mr Ingham describes their requests. And 'if people do not believe' in the innocence of his agreement to help, 'that is their problem.'

Springing a Leak

LAST WEEK *Press Gang* began with a paean of praise for Adam Raphael of the *Observer* who anticipated the contents of the Franks Falklands Report by forty-eight hours. Mr Raphael's coup would have no place in a column which, today, deals with leaks, were it not for one extraordinary aspect of his exclusive story. For the triumphant author argued that he had no prior knowledge of the report's contents, but simply pieced together the opinions of sundry witnesses and came to the conclusion that their evidence would exonerate the Prime Minister.

Now that we have all had the opportunity to digest the Franks Report, Mr Raphael's achievement seems even more spectacular. For after weeks of careful sifting, *he actually came to the same conclusion as the document's two final paragraphs.* The rest of Franks — as all the serious newspapers have now explained — is highly critical of the Government's performance. It takes a journalist of real talent to conduct an independent enquiry and come up, not with the opinions expressed in the body of the report which his investigations mirrored, but with the conflicting judgement with which it ended.

But as Mr Raphael's story was not based on the sight of a secret document it is not part of this week's subject. Today we examine the publication of private papers: the sort of thing that I vividly remember from my days in the Cabinet. All Cabinets leak. And I suspect that all low-grade Cabinet Ministers react as I always reacted to the Prime Minister's Thursday-morning denunciation of the known but unnamed culprit. I always feared that although I was wholly innocent, I was the principal suspect. The intonation, the choice of pronouns and the careful textual analysis of the offending extract all pointed to me.

No doubt someone at New Scotland Yard felt very much the same on the Monday morning after the *Mail on Sunday* published its 'EXCLUSIVE: On a plan to devolve the police'. Certainly the story made Fleet Street buzz. For it was written by Chester Stern, Crime Correspondent. And not only is Chester Stern a real person, he is an ex-information officer of the Metropolitan Police. It was assumed that Mr Stern was in the know. So his story was dutifully copied into the rival editions of other papers. Unfortunately, he grossly overdramatized the proposals. Innocent politicians who were booked for television and radio broadcasts on the strength of his mountain were told that they were not wanted when the Commissioner of Police unveiled his mouse.

All hope that a second David Henke had been discovered was extinguished. When David Henke was local government correspondent of the *Guardian* he seemed to reveal the contents of a secret document almost every day. They usually belonged to the Department of the Environment, and concerned matters of immense controversy and even greater complication. 'Rate Support Grant Formula to be Changed' he would prophesy. And then would follow a passage of explanation which appeared to be written in code. When translated into English the prophecies always turned out to be correct.

Mr Henke clearly benefited from the activities of a mole — a man or woman, deep inside the DoE, who surfaced from time to time bearing a piece of paper. Most leaks are by word of mouth — which is why so many of them turn out to be inaccurate. A perfect example of the fallibility of leaks and the frailty of leakers is to be found in the spate of stories concerning the Government's new immigration proposals. Knowing Conservative backbenchers have stopped lobby correspondents in House of Commons corridors and assured them (in absolute confidence) that they know the Home Secretary's secret intentions. The lobby correspondents have confused confidentiality with authority and a lot of them will be proved wrong. They have all been sprinkled by conflicting leaks.

The other problem about leaks is that they are usually spurted out for a purpose. There are in Parliament and the Civil Service genuine enuretics who leak because they cannot help it, contemptible and compulsive blabbers who cannot see a journalist without wanting to reveal a secret. But most leakers relieve themselves for a purpose. The people in the Department of Health who spread around papers which outlined plans for re-organizing the Health Service did it because they believed re-organization to be synonymous with destruction. Stories from the Cabinet are usually spread with the specific purpose of discrediting one faction and promoting another.

In my experience leaks rarely do any harm and are the cause of much innocent fun. Occasionally they do positive good — as in the case of President Nixon's destruction. More often they do no more than prick the bubble of a politician's self esteem. For nothing makes a Minister feel more important than knowing something that the rest of us do not know. Hence all the fuss when a story which was intended for release on a Monday morning appears in the newspapers on the previous Friday. The leak is also the enemy of news manipulation. If the careful plan requires a story simultaneously to explode on every front page and it pops up prematurely in a single paper, the people who planned the megaton presentation are naturally furious. They take refuge in pompous pronouncements about the proprieties of public life.

This is how the Government responded to that very special category of leak, the broken embargo, when the list of Falklands War gallantry awards was broadcast twenty-four hours before official publication date. Newspapers and television companies had been given an early sight of the names, so that they could prepare their articles in advance. Falkland enthusiasm prompted some of them to jump the gun. The official complaint was not that another reminder of the Government's victory had been dissipated but that the families of medallists had been pestered at the wrong time.

Of course, the more the Government tries to manage the news, the more good journalists determine to tap the leaks. Which brings us back to Adam Raphael's story in the *Observer* — or rather would bring us back to it, if we suspected that the ingenious Mr Raphael had actually caught early sight of the Franks Report.

Once A Week

My Funny Valentine

THIRTY YEARS AGO I held a highly simplistic view of women's magazines. The glossy and expensive publications I associated with romance and adventure. And I genuinely believed that I would meet the haughty subjects of their fashion plates as soon as I bought a new suit from Burtons. The poor relations of *Harpers, Queen,* and *Vogue* I assumed to be obsessed with marriage, homes and babies. I imagined that their columns were made up of knitting patterns, sentimental fiction and horoscopes.

My opinion of publications which, sociologists insisted, had done more to emancipate the working girl than the combined efforts of Emily Pankhurst and Marie Stopes, was compounded by the experiences of a friend. Fearful of telling his family that he had grown bored with his thesis, *Heine as a Literary Critic*, he wrote to other refugees from post-graduate scholarship hoping to find acceptable reasons for deserting the duller groves of academe.

He received only two replies. One was from a man whose PhD starved to death for want of sustaining original material. His title asked the question, *Could Goethe Swim?* The second academic casualty had been examining *The Underlying Values in Women's Magazines.* After six months of intensive study she was suddenly overcome by an irresistible urge to fall in love, marry and live happily ever after.

Her brain was washed during a more innocent age — the days when virginity was never lost in print and young doctors always had square jaws and honourable intentions. That was before the new wave of women's magazines washed across the bookstalls; bringing with it *Cosmopolitan's* cult of hormones, haemoglobin and hysterectomies. It was also before Audrey Slaughter invented *Over 21,* a magazine that claims to reject both the tradition of moon, June and orange blossom and more modern demands for fair shares in sexual satisfaction.

The February edition is not at all the sort of magazine that Robert Herrick would have enjoyed reading to his son on Valentine's Day. An article by Celia Haddon begins with the highly unseasonable assertion that 'sex is not fun' and goes on to suggest that 'Like other hobbies, the pursuit and collection of sexual combinations takes up surplus time and requires a great deal of skill, dedication and ingenuity.' Readers shocked by Ms Haddon's *The Limits of Sex* may find release in future issues. We are promised extracts from *Night Thoughts,* the 'Reflections of a Sex Therapist' by Avodah K. Offit, MD. Rumours that Dr Offit invented aversion therapy are unfounded.

But much of *Over 21* is far less silly than a quick glance at such articles make it seem. It is produced in the belief that few of its readers will waste a hard-earned 50p on advice about how to make men feel good when they get home from a hard day's work. Nor is it a magazine for teenagers, with interests limited to the cheap route to high fashion and the way in which Adam and the Ants spend their spare time. It aims its sights at intelligent adult women, who work, wash their own hair, go shopping in comfortable shoes and fantasize a little.

For them romance, as conventionally defined, is a bit of a joke. Of course Pronuptia offers readers a 'beautiful beginning from as little as £49.95'. But there is little in the magazine itself to suggest that even a decent girl's aim is aisle and altar. 'Would You Make a Perfect Bride?' seems unlikely to drum up business for the shops which cater for 'those very precious moments'. Question 13, in that quiz, asks the reader if she thinks that Germaine Greer has (a) been influential, (b) some good arguments, (c) written *The Female Eunuch,* (d) nice hair.

Over 21 thinks that its appeal lies in its infinite variety. So, as well as the sociology and the gentle debunking of love and marriage, it contains a horoscope which is not supposed to be ridiculous despite its prediction that before January 19th 'Venus will have backed into Capricorn'. When that conjunction occurs, the gored goddess will no doubt be grateful for the services of 'The Raymond Young Private Clinic — buttock firming and tightening' a speciality. Mr Young finances one of the more bizarre items in the classified columns of a magazine that clearly takes as eclectic a view of its advertisements as it does of its features. If *Over 21* is really read by more than a million readers (each copy passing through eight pairs of hands), there is little wonder that Atrixo skin lotion buys a full colour double-page spread. But it is more difficult to understand why such a profitable paper should wish to take money from Appleby Nash who offers '300 ways to spice up your love life'.

If the advertisements are any guide to *Over 21* opinions, emotionally mature young ladies believe that clean hair and clear skins are the real secrets of sexual success. But nowhere in the pages that promote the idea of more body and life in the coiffure and less bristle and fluff on the legs is there the slightest suggestion that the preening and primping is done with the object of increasing male attraction.

Catching and keeping is not an *Over 21* preoccupation. Indeed, a careful study of Ms Haddon's controversial work reveals that she believes that sex 'pays off' best when it creates a sense of mutual belonging. Sentimentalists will rejoice that a magazine exists to cater for the female halves of equal partnerships and enjoys so much success that IPC is soon to publish *Options*, its own variation on the same theme. And I have heard both youths and virgins say that all the conventional chat about mates and coupling with Valentines went out with Robert Herrick. *Over 21* is on to a good thing.

Spectator Sport

IF I AM biased about the *Spectator*, my prejudice is in its favour. When, during the days of its Gower Street glory, I entered its romantically dilapidated offices to deliver an 'Endpiece' or a 'View from the Left', I always felt that Addison and Steele were following me up the ricketty staircase. With Ian Macleod in command (and the present editor of the *Sunday Telegraph* kept in an upstairs room to do business with the like of me) the *Spectator* was usually interesting, often amusing and sometimes even elegant.

True, it was prone to the near fatal inclination to sell itself to rich eccentrics. And each trainee proprietor seemed afflicted by an insane determination to hire a new editor with more baroque manners and a more florid style than those affected by the previous owner's nominee. But a magazine that can survive Nigel Lawson and George Gale in quick succession must possess heroic virtues.

With Alexander Chancellor in charge, it has become once more the most readable of the political weeklies. If that comparative praise was the best we could bestow,it might not be much of a compliment. For *The Economist* increasingly seeks to prove that jargon is the essential complement to its racy layout and cute headlines; the *New Statesman* clearly believes that decent English is a manifestation of bourgeois values, and *Tribune* is simply ire and anger broken down into lines and paragraphs.

But the *Spectator* does not simply shine like a polished sentence in an illiterate world. It is, by any standards, remarkably (and consistently) well written. It contains essays; not columns or reports, but carefully constructed articles that combine fact and opinion. Indeed, were it not for its intolerable political opinions, the *Spectator* would be a pleasure to read. And that is not all.

The back of the paper provides valuable out-door relief for journalists down on their luck. It helps to supplement the inadequate salary that *Private Eye* rightly pays to Richard Ingrams. Its book reviews allow Enoch Powell occasionally to remind us that he was once a scholar, not a demagogue. And Ferdinand Mount writes about politics with an elan which none of his competitors can match. For all that I give thanks. However, my gratitude does not extend to the Paul Johnson column.

Mr Johnson writes each week about the Press — a difficult enough task even for a journalist who struggles for objectivity. For instance, an acknowledged socialist writing about a conservative magazine would be treated with proper suspicion if he denounced it line by line. And a rabid reactionary — with the cleansing zeal Savonarola might have shown had he been a late convert to political purification — would not be trusted to give a fair break to the radical *Guardian* or the Labour-saving *Mirror*.

Mr Johnson overcomes the occupational hazard of suspected bias by abandoning all pretence of balance and objectivity. Usually, he does not write a real Press column at all. He writes about politics, interspersing his prejudices with an occasional reference to, or quotation from, a newspaper. His obsession is Press freedom and the hidden menace of state socialist censorship.

'Monitor Needed' provided a perfect example of style and context. 'The Far Left,' Mr Johnson explained, 'is particularly active and audacious in the field of media studies . . . There may be media academics who are not Marxists of one kind or another, if so I'd like to know them." What is more, 'NUJ penetration of the BBC news and documentary services . . . is proceeding fast.' Even the management has become contaminated as a result of 'the shift to the left within independent TV caused by the re-allocation of contracts by Lady Plowden and her gang.'

When three weeks later, his column was called 'Paranoid' I first took it to be a recantation of his earlier view that 'objective news gathering agencies' like ITN are being 'harrassed' by augmented campaigns of complaint and criticism. But I was mistaken. He was complaining about an *Observer* diary column that mentioned him. No irony was intended when he wrote that it is a 'pity that those whose professional duties ought to breed a healthy scepticism should be so eager to deal in fantasies about their own industry.'

'The Big Read' (published on January 23rd) actually used the word 'journalist' in the first sentence. But it was not the trumpet of a prophesy that a real article about newspapers could not be far behind. The second sentence was an attack on Michael Foot and by the end of the offering the reader is back in the familiar groove. Lenin's belief that he had a mission 'to interpret the will of the proletariat' is 'similar' to the attitude of the 'Bennite movement'. Leninism 'ultimately ended in all the horrors'. *Ergo* . . .

Three of Mr Johnson's January articles were written in a similar state of apprehensive excitement. Hope that, like Hamlet, he would begin to tell a hawk from a handsaw when the weather changes was extinguished in the *Spectator's* first February issue. 'Brother Blue Pencil' concerned the 'attempted censorship of four British newspapers by members of ASLEF'. I regard the train drivers' brief refusal to carry the *Sun* and its sister papers as both foolish and wrong. But no balanced article could have leaped from that unhappy episode to: 'curbing the Press was Lenin's first decisive act when he took power in 1917 . . . if Benn wants the unions to censor the Press, it is just as well we should know now rather than later'.

In criticizing Paul Johnson's column I am of course open to two charges. The first is political prejudice: the desire to suppress criticism of the Labour Party. On that count there is not sufficient evidence for the prosecution to proceed with its case. The second indictment is that I am a rival columnist writing on the same subject in a competing magazine. To that, I plead guilty as charged, offering (in extenuation) the advice to beware of substitutes and always to choose the genuine article. But there is more to it than that. I remain an admirer of the *Spectator*. And I grieve when one of its contributors holds it up to ridicule.

Sermons of the Mount

FERDINAND MOUNT IS a gent. As well as possessing a gent's name, and benefiting from a gent's education (Eton and Christ Church), he wears gents' suits (well-cut tweed) when he travels to Scottish by-elections and works for the *Spectator,* a gents' paper. Most important of all, he has a gent's face. It is that special shade of pink that comes from moderate exposure to fresh air and the lifelong freedom from pimples and acne that only careful upbringing guarantees. It shines out of the Press Gallery in the House of Commons, from within a sea of features and complexions that the laws of libel, the conventions of Parliament and the hope of political survival all prevent me from describing in detail. He is also — according to the few fellow correspondents who know him well — a very nice man.

In many ways he always seems to me the Peter Carrington of political journalists — consciously (though effortlessly) elegant and diffident in the manner of a man who feels no need to prove that he is right. That moral and intellectual certainty has made Mount an independent voice amongst political commentators. It may well — as in Carrington's case — have encouraged him into making a disastrous decision.

42

Ferdinand Mount is about to become the head of the Prime Minister's Policy Unit. I do not believe that he will feel at home there.

At first, 'getting on' with Mrs Thatcher will pose no insuperable problems. I have no doubt that he is invariably and naturally courteous to ladies — even grocers' daughters with vulgar opinions. But once inside Number 10 the indignities will come not singly but in battalions. He may be required to offer advice to Norman Tebbit, a man whose chief contribution to the Conservative Party is the provision of living proof that Tories no longer need to be gentlemen. Educating uncouth Ministers in the corridors of Mrs Thatcher's power may not prove so easy as rebuking them in the columns of the *Spectator* and the *Standard*.

And that is what Mr Mount will be required to do. For he has not been recruited to deal with the Press but to advise on policy. Keeping Fleet Street in line will remain the exclusive responsibility of Bernard Ingham, an ex-*Guardian* Labour correspondent turned Department of Energy civil servant, who has made a long, but nevertheless remarkable, transition from Labour Party enthusiast to spokesman for a Tory Prime Minister. Mr Ingham also has a red face. But it is a proper Yorkshire working-class red face of a sort that is much revered in this column. Side by side Mr Ingham and Mr Mount could illustrate a learned work entitled *The Physiological Identification of Class Origins*.

I have not decided if Mr Ingham's opinions have changed since the days when I knew him well or if he just suppresses his inclination to contradict everything that Mrs Thatcher says. In either event, he ought to give Mr Mount some advice about how to survive without actually agreeing with the Prime Minister. For his job will be to provide alternative advice — the opinion of a clear, uncluttered mind that the Civil Service is too stuffy or timid to utter. On the evidence of his writing, Mr Mount is neither the Prime Minister's spiritual surrogate nor her intellectual clone.

A year ago, when law and order was close to every Tory heart, Mr Mount wrote in the *Standard* that 'For the first time in this country, the conduct of the police is being brought into question, not amongst parts of the working class who might regard themselves as the hereditary enemies of the constabulary, but among the respectable middle classes.' Neither Margaret Thatcher nor Willie Whitelaw will accept that from me. I hope that they will accept it from the new head of the Policy Unit.

And his interest in constabulary duties persists. On March 27th he wrote in the *Spectator* an account of the Government's Parliamentary claims about the crime rate — 'The Prime Minister havered and stumbled, groped for the number of murders, couldn't find it . . . and finally grasped gratefully at the lifebelt, to wit, that it has nothing to do with the Government.' If I judge the PM's character aright, Mr Mount's appointment proves that she does not read the *Spectator*. And if I know anything about the civil servants who will be competing with Mr Mount for her ear, she will soon be presented with a red-box filled with carefully marked back numbers.

Included in it will be his advice on the Budget — 'If this is to be a Budget "for" any specific category, both moral duty and political prudence (in whatever order you fancy) suggest that it should be a Budget not for business but for the unemployed.' Of course, the Prime Minister took no notice. But she has now clasped a wet to her bosom.

I hope, for Mr Mount's sake, that when she finds out she will not tear up his contract before his startled eyes. Such an incident would amuse connoisseurs of life's ironies. For Dr Bernard Donoghue — the head of the Policy Unit under Wilson and Callaghan, who moved in the other direction from politics to journalism — ended his career at *The Times* with Rupert Murdoch publicly shredding his indentures. But if that happens there will, for the rest of us, be one consolation.

Mr Mount will be writing again. And that seems to me a highly desirable state of affairs. Proust quoted in an attack on the Leader of the Opposition. Support for a speech by me preceded by an admission of how painful he found it to accept that I was right about anything. Jokes about Sir Arthur Bryant. Nothing is sacred to Mr Mount. And his sacrilege is always elegantly (though I suspect not effortlessly) written. I hope that Mrs Thatcher appreciates well-written internal memorandums. Otherwise he will be entirely wasted.

Avid Listener

THE LISTENER IS a splendid magazine. There may be cynical readers of this essentially idealistic column who think that I have come to that conclusion after the exercise of biased judgement. They will be right. But the bias is not quite the prejudice that many of them will expect. It is true that I wrote 114 consecutive columns for the paper. But I ended my happy association with BBC Publications only partly because of my life-long infatuation with the *Guardian*. I feared that *The Listener* was going to change, and not for the better. I was wrong. Despite my vested interest in vindication, I repeat the refutation of my gloomy judgement. *The Listener* is a splendid magazine.

Critics of *The Listener* say that it survives on subsidy and that it enjoys an unfair advantage over the *New Statesman* and the *Spectator* because its income is padded by subventions from the television licence fee. Of course that is partly true. But one of the strengths of *The Listener* is the subsidy that nobody talks about — the ability to print articles of real value because expensive authors have broadcast something along the same lines for the BBC.

I am not Bernard Levin's most devoted admirer. But I do understand that my reservations represent a minority position. I also know that to commission him to write a nine-part series on the pleasures of life — with each pleasure running to nearly three thousand words — would cost a great deal more than the generality of liberal arts magazines could afford. But there he is in *The Listener* each week, indulging himself in the way that his devotees so admire. The secret is, of course, the spoken word in print. The old Reithian justification for *The Listener* is also the reason why it can boast so many big names on its front page. The BBC pays for the broadcast and the BBC magazine gets first refusal and early sight of transcript. Long may it so continue.

Of course, not all *The Listener*'s treasures are bought second-hand from Portland Place. Under Tony Howard's editorship it expanded the space devoted to book reviews. Indeed, it elevated its literary pages into an institution in their own right — the *Listener* Review of Books. Perhaps it is the romantic appeal of the BBC's old cultural connection —

Spanish Civil War poets working for the Overseas Service and Malcolm Muggeridge pretending to be profound on the *Brains Trust* that makes the approaches of literary editor Derwent May irresistible. Whatever the secret of his success (and it is certainly not the price he pays) in the last two weeks of July he managed to recruit D.J. Enwright, John Vaizey, Paul Johnson, Marghanita Laski, D.A.N. Jones, Kate Cruise O'Brien and J.R. Pole. August began with P.N. Furbank and Clancy Sigal.

My fear was that the new editor, Russell Twisk — marathon runner and *Radio Times* executive — would change all that. He certainly arrived at Marylebone High Street determined to include within his paper a section on next week's broadcasting. Until his day the paper almost always looked back to last week's programmes. His Viewer/Listener Guide looks ahead. I have no way of judging the success of his supplement. Its effects on circulation will not be certain for several months. And I cannot climb inside the mind of people who want a preview of Dr Anthony Clare (from the Institute of Psychiatry) bringing 'the insinuating skills of his profession to the media game of interviewing'. But what I do know is that trailers for 'instant history lessons' and 'TV-computerized show business' have not diminished the rest of the paper.

Certainly Mr Twisk has made changes. He has wisely kept Peter Brooke's excellent cover cartoon. But he has incorporated pictures into his texts. Frances Donnelly on Bloomsbury (to turn R.H. Tawney upside down, not the pleasant London district but the silly London set) is enlivened by beautiful pictures of Vanessa Bell and Virginia Woolf. The BBC library is stuffed with such historical gems and it is obviously *The Listener's* duty to publish them for our general pleasure. However, whether it is necessary to print Gerald Kaufman's portrait in the middle of his 'Centrepiece' essay ('... Yorkshire boyhood. Roy Hattersley had better get it into his head that he has no monopoly in that line of country') is quite a different consideration.

The regular reviewers — television, radio, music — have had the little cartoons removed from the tops of their columns. But their space has been protected — fifteen hundred words for television, a thousand for radio and sometimes almost two thousand for music. The pages of criticism alone — books and other arts combined — make *The Listener* worth its 50p cover price. And as a bonus it still wages its campaign to popularize the light essay in the minds of literate readers. When my 'Endpieces' ended last January, Mr Twisk initially confirmed my fears by cutting the feature down to half its original size and employing well-known personalities to write it on a monthly rota. I thought the result was horrific. But Mr Twisk has more than made up for his initial error.

'Centrepiece' — which immediately follows some of the best written and best informed letters sent to any English publication — is always an essay of the old discursive school. Mr Twisk may have issued a general instruction to contributors or he may simply have recruited people of a proper turn of mind. But whatever the cause, the result is a whole page which fascinates because of style rather than content. Indeed, the more inconsequential the subject the better the writing. For the essayist has to catch and keep the reader's interest with the quality of his prose. There are few places which indulge such elegant pleasures and *The Listener* ought to be encouraged for that as well as for its other many virtues. I do not suggest that it ought to be your favourite weekly magazine. But if you can afford two periodicals it ought to be your second choice.

City Slickers

THE ECONOMIST INSISTS that it is a newspaper not a magazine. Ever since Walter Bagehot's distinguished and unpronounceable period as editor it has chosen that humble and inappropriate description. But no one should imagine that its willingness to share a generic title with the *Camden and St Pancras Chronicle* and the *Worksop Guardian* is an indication of innate modesty about its importance and accomplishments. *The Economist* is the paper of smart people, for smart people. It is that quality which makes it so popular in America, where its circulation has trebled in four years.

Indeed, during the first six months of 1982, more copies were sold in the US of A than in the UK of GB and NI. Out of a total circulation of 212,000 copies, 70,000 fell through corporate letter-boxes in New York, were flung into white wooden porches in Baton Rouge or landed on squirrel-infested front lawns in Baltimore. In the United States *The Economist* is a wow. Indeed, for many Americans who pride themselves on their knowledge of the world, *The Economist* is the word, the truth and the light about what goes on beyond the weekly meetings of their local Council on International Relations.

Which is in some ways a pity. For the picture that *The Economist* paints of Britain is not always typical of our life and times. It is particularly incompetent in its coverage of labour (or perhaps we should say labor) relations. It has long been obsessed by the trade unions' responsibility for our economic collapse. Over a dozen years ago it developed a theory that the post-war boom ended with the Government's agreement to pay the railwaymen the extra one per cent that made the difference between strike and continued operation. But it is not only its judgement which is often at fault. Sometimes it gets the facts wrong.

In 1981, when every political and industrial correspondent in London was guesstimating the trade union vote for Denis Healey and Tony Benn during their rival campaigns for the Labour Party's Deputy Leadership, *The Economist* prophesied that Tom Jackson's Union of Communication Workers would go for Benn. It had already gone for Healey. And the error of fact was only part of the mistake. Anyone who imagined that Mr Jackson and his postmen would desert Healey ought not to be employed on writing about politics or the trade unions. The same stricture applies to last week's judgement about the TUC Congress. 'The Brighton jamboree', it wrote, 'will be cluttered by rhetoric in support of the health workers' dispute.' The clear implication of the pejorative use of the word rhetoric was that the old cart-horse would be all words and no action. In fact, there was almost unanimous agreement to a one-day strike.

It is not simply prejudice that leads *The Economist* into such errors. Its political position has always meant that it stood at arm's length from the unions — ever since, under its previous editor Alastair Burnet, it spoke for Edward Heath and the new Conservatism of manufacturing industry, wall-to-wall carpet and Brahms on the 'music-centre' inside the antique-type cabinet. The real problem is that *The Economist* cannot help admiring its own reflection in the water. And occasionally it falls in with an embarrassing splash.

Such charges could not be levelled against the *Investors Chronicle* (and *Financial World*). That extraordinary magazine seems to go out of its way to make itself unreadable. It claims to be 'the financial weekly that really means business', but both its prose and style and typography suggest that only the determinedly dull and the triumphantly tedious are likely to succeed in industry and commerce. Consider a sentence from Sue Landau, the editor of a survey on enterprise zones. 'The new map is a familiar sight after the two-year interval between being proposed when Sir Keith Joseph was in charge at the D.O.I, and its introduction in August, although some areas won reprieves from downgrading or were upgraded by the Department's review.'

It is extraordinary that a magazine that is to involve Brian Reading should allow such assaults on the English language. In his previous incarnations, Mr Reading was credited with the passage in one of Mr Heath's election handouts that promised to 'cut prices at a stroke' and is also said to be the man who invented the word 'slumpflation'. But such flights of descriptive fancy are not the *Investors Chronicle* style. 'Can rental growth justify yields?' it asks. And 'US defence drive should restore Dowty's glamour', it asserts. The *Investors Chronicle* seems to make its readers work hard as a matter of principle.

The Economist chooses quite the opposite style. It invented the cute coloured cover; emblazoned with pictures of models of politicians, cartoons and puns that are more arresting than informative. 'Wizardry my dear Watson,' it observes over a photograph of Sherlock Holmes, 'using science to catch crooks.' Its first half-dozen pages of what amount to editorials are always unapologetically didactic and consciously clever. 'Hong Kong isn't Port Stanley,' we are reminded. 'The governments of the United States and the European community ... must be amusing the ghosts of both Groucho and Karl Marx,' we are informed with a startling lack of originality. And yet, and yet . . .

The 'and yets' all concern the so-called surveys which follow the home news. The pages on America — still under the influence though no longer formally controlled by John Midgley, the long-time Washington bureau chief — are really required reading for any 'Britisher' who wants to understand 'the States'. And the pages of financial analysis which follow are detailed and digestible accounts of what is going on in the world. In fact, *The Economist* creates the impression that the talented Andrew Knight (who has been editor since an indecently early age) sells his paper on its first dozen pages and maintains his intellectual self-respect in the rest of the paper.

Not a bad trick — as one of his own front pages might have put it.

King and Country

AT ONLY 70p for over 450 grammes of paper, it is clearly the best value on the news stands, if bulk is to be the criterion of magazine merit. The *Spectator* costs five pence less, but it tips the scale at only ten per cent of *Country Life's* weight. And *Country Life* exudes an air of quality as well as quantity. It has class as well as bulk — like the 'mahogany side cupboard with black fossil limestone top — probably German *c*1810. 5ft. 5½in wide £982' which appeared in Frank Davis's 'Talking About Salesrooms' column.

'Talking About Salesrooms' caught my mood exactly as I took my usual advantage of W.H. Smith's unconscious hospitality and flicked aimlessly through the shelves of glossy magazines with which that company tempts the unwary. 'My first reaction,' Mr Davies wrote, 'was what a lump of pompous rotundity! Coming back to it a few moments later, I rebuked myself for such a snap judgement and began to see much virtue in it.' He wrote about the mahogany side cupboard. I thought of *Country Life*.

It is, of course, impossible not to be infatuated by its covers. On April 15th, Wells Cathedral was set against a slate-grey sky and reflected in still, green, Somerset water. I admit to being addicted to English churches, English fields, English hills, English castles and English manor houses. But *Country Life* covers even manage to make abroad seem attractive. The special French number in May 1979 made a French château look comparable with Harewood House. The October 23rd issue in 1980 featured winter travel and included a picture of the palm trees that was almost alluring.

And both the faithful portrayal of England's magnificence and the photographic legerdemain that makes assorted foreign parts seem as beautiful continues inside the coloured covers. Even the advertisements conform to the same high pictorial standards. Mappin and Webb offer 'a masterpiece in the tradition of another century' in such clear focus, that the prospective purchaser can read the name on the knifeblade. It is, of course, 'Sheffield', the only mark consistent with a claim about classic cutlery.

However, the pictures aside, it is easy to be put off by the pompous rotundity to which — in another context — Frank Davis took proper exception.

'A hen's egg laced with strychnine may be just as lethal to the child who picks it up as to the crow or fox for which it was intended,' the editorial reminds everyone foolish enough to overlook such an obvious hazard.

'My photograph shows a portrait of a woman painted by Sir Oswald Bailey,' writes Mrs Doepel of Lincoln. ' I wonder if any of your readers can tell me her true identity.' But be not dismayed. The items really only suitable for Women's Institute lectures are overshelmingly outnumbered by articles of real fascination.

Last week, the three-page article on the conservation of Wells Cathedral was written with such rigorous concentration on the subject that it did not include a picture of that extraordinary Cathedral's cross-over arches that meet in mid-air above choir and transept like great stone saltires. But I defy any reader with even a moderately lively mind not to be captivated by Richard Haskin's account of the way in which 'the chivalry of heaven', arranged in niches on the West front, is being restored.

I suppose it is the advertisements for improbable houses,

through which the prospective reader has to plough, that create the initial alienating impression of stockbroker sensitivities. No doubt it is the income from Knight Frank & Rutley no less than the full colour contributions from Asbach Brandy and Courvoisier that helps to keep the cover price at 70p. And last week there were certainly a lot of des. props. on the market. Not that *Country Life* estate agents stoop to such penny-pinching abbreviations. If, like Savills of Edinburgh, you are selling Glenaff Castle by private treaty you list the amenities of the 'luxuriously decorated' Scottish 'baronial home' in detail.

And of course, some of the feature articles seem specially designed for lairds with baronial homes to decorate or lords with space on their walls to be filled with '17th Century Embroidery Depicting Charlie's Escape after the battle of Worcester in 1651, 20in wide £1,150' or 'Miniature of Fanny Burney by John Bogle, 1783, 3¼in high £6,500'. I am no more likely to bid for either than I am to buy a 'silver-mounted cucumber slicer *c*1790 8½in length, £500'. But such glimpses at portable property from an earlier age have a special fascination for the social voyeur. For readers who take their social history more seriously, there are genuinely serious articles.

I wonder if Miss Karen Ann Beale enjoyed the four page feature on 'the career and patronage of Ralph, Lord Cromwell, the builder of Wingfield Manor,' which was published on April 15th together with 'plans of the apartments in the West tower'. My interest in the young lady's archaeological enthusiasms was stimulated by her full-page photograph. It decorated the first editorial page in the same issue. Like the *Country Life* notes on the 'siege of Jalalabal, Afghanistan 1841-2' and sketch of James, Duke of Monmouth — 'the Protestant duke as sportsman', the portrait of the recently betrothed Miss Beale has a timeless quality.

Miss Anna Steele (who similarly graced the first editorial page when the Afghan notes were published) and Miss Catrin Robert (whose thrilling magazine exposure coincided with the tercentenary, in 1979, of Monmouth's fall from grace) are, to me at least, virtually indistinguishable from Miss Beale, the most recent *Country Life* equivalent of a centre-fold, playmate, or bunny of the month. No doubt their doting parents — not to mention the gallants to whom their troths were plighted — will deeply resent the implication that they are pleasant but unexceptional girls and say that since they were selected from a bevy of weekly volunteers for Establishment exposure, they must have some sort of special grace. I simply regret that they give such a prejudicial first impression about *Country Life*. Further on, as Mr Davies would say, there is much virtue in it.

Altered Statesman

CLICHES ARE NOT allowed in this column. So we welcome the arrival of Charles Wintour's fortnightly *Observer* Press review without making any mention of imitation being the sincerest form of that unctuous attitude which (at least with decent people) gets you nowhere. Mr Wintour began by attacking what, in the language of war, would be called a soft target — the *Mail on Sunday*.

Excoriating the execrable is the critic's occasional obligation and sometimes even his pleasure. Describing the slow death of a once-great weekly journal can never be anything but a dolorous duty. But if there is the prospect of reincarnation, the burden weighs less heavily. That, let us all profoundly hope, is the prospect for the *New Statesman*.

I confess that I have not bought the *New Statesman* for years — and it is even longer since I last read it regularly. For some months after the revolution wrought in between its covers by Bruce Page, its editor between 1978 and 1982, I continued to take delivery for reasons concerned with loyalty and inertia. But I gradually abandoned reading it as, to me at least, it became literally unreadable. Part of the problem was the agit-prop layout — the little items of information confined within their own square boxes. An additional offence was the bizarre topics chosen as the subject of supplementary features — a crime against the tradition of weekly journalism compounded by an obsession with tables and graphs.

Peter Kellner, recruited by Page from the *Sunday Times*,

analyses political ebbs and flows more lucidly than any other contemporary commentator. But his skills are essentially numerate rather than literate. His predecessors as political correspondent — Tony Howard, Gerald Kaufman, Alan Watkins, Matt Coady and James Fenton — never descended to statistics. But Mr Page seemed to believe that elegant writing was an anachronism, as unfitted to the world of microchips and word processors as Arthur Marshall, crossword puzzles and chess competitions — all three of which institutions were removed during the Page purge.

Two months ago, I began to buy the *New Statesman* again. For its new editor, Hugh Stephenson, is a man who once managed to make the business columns of *The Times* entertaining and, more recently, contributed to *Guardian* editorials; the best written (if not always the most intellectually consistent) leaders in Fleet Street. Mr Stephenson is in the great tradition of socialist gentlemen — Winchester, Oxford, Royal Navy, Foreign Office and Putney Constituency Labour Party. He shows no sign of being an avid demonstrator of feeling passionately about the protest movement. The Great Turnstile staff did not want him to become editor.

They may be relieved — if not reconciled to his appointment — by the way in which he has behaved during the early weeks of his stewardship. Certainly the paper has recently seemed to show some respect for decent writing — Ralf Dahrendorf on the Crosland biography and William Shawcross on the latest instalment of the Kissinger memoirs. But the front of the paper retains its essential extra-mural quality. In a single issue he published 'Women in Retreat' (based on a survey carried out by the Sociological Research Unit at University College, Cardiff), 'A Surge of Labour Feminists' and 'Black Women Organise . . . and Divide'.

But the journalists who sprayed aerosol on the office walls to signify their disappointment that their editorial nominee had been turned down, ought not to assume that their war against literacy has been won. Mr Stephenson is a yachtsman. And he knows the importance of tacking into the wind. The likelihood is that when autumn comes the *New Statesman* will begin to show some changes. Though whether or not it will fill the gap on our news stands that ought to be occupied by what the Americans would call a 'liberal arts magazine' is by no means as certain. Mr Stephenson does not, apparently, share Mr Page's belief that a political journal should contain a fact in every line. But he has an unhealthy respect for figures and reservations about old-style political comments of the sort that once filled the paper.

He has, however, brought back the editorial. So the *New Statesman* once again publishes the collegiate opinions which were abandoned in the anarchic days of his predecessor. The leader appears on page two, as its traditional home on the cover is now occupied by a picture, which is allowed to waste enough space for a thousand trenchant words in the belief that it will beckon from the bookstalls to casual customers and seduce them into a sudden purchase. Whether or not a serious political weekly attracts business in that way is a question that has yet to be conclusively answered. Indeed, nobody is quite sure of who the potential new readers are. There lies Mr Stephenson's dilemma.

New Statesman readership now stands at about 33,000. When Dick Crossman became editor, almost a decade ago, 88,000 copies were sold each week. It may be that the steady decline (most of it taking place before Bruce Page's arrival) cut the total readership down to the hard-core of inseparables. Or it may be that Mr Page saved the paper by recruiting a whole army of brand-new readers who took the place of the traditional *New Statesman* devotees. Mr Page's defenders (who still abound on the paper) say that the demand for Kingsley Martin and J.B. Priestley died with the creation of the polytechnics. Without Page turning over a new leaf, the paper would no longer exist — or so they claim.

If Mr Stephenson accepts that analysis, nothing much will change at Great Turnstile. Siren voices will certainly whisper that the pocket-calculator-carrying readers of the 1980s do not want a return to style and comment. They come to their own judgements about politicians by watching *Question Time*. They have ready-made opinions on every political topic. And they are certainly unmoved by standards of literacy. I harbour hopes that Mr Stephenson will not be lured on to the rocks of statistical disaster. The autumn is the proper season for making great changes in weekly magazines.

For it is when evenings begin to draw in that readers lightly turn to thoughts of film reviews and literary criticism. Let us hope that Mr Stephenson catches that tide and charts a course towards making the *New Statesman* readable again.

Nine Tenths of the Law

Eyes Down

I BLAME RUPERT MURDOCH. True, the rival *Daily Star* was the first national (or nearly national) newspaper to go into the bingo business. But the numbers game is only an extension of the notion that circulation is best increased by the hard sell of novelties rather than news. And the *Sun's* strident campaigns — built around sudden bursts of multi-coloured television frenzy — pioneered the mass sale of cheap rubbish as a way of attracting buyers if not readers. Those were the days when Sir Larry Lamb became the knight of the garter, the exotic bra, the frilly knickers and the novelty suspender belt. Since then, popular newspapers have increasingly thought of themselves as merchandise to be packaged and marketed with the help of 'special offers'.

Of course, there have been 'special offers' of a sort for years. In my childhood we did not read the paper that would have helped us to acquire sets of English classic novels or cheap insurance. But the box Brownie which took all the out-of-focus pictures of me astride a Bridlington donkey came into our possession with the help of coupons cut from the *John Bull* magazine. As we took our summer snapshots on northern beaches, we felt that we had no hope of successfully challenging a passer-by with the unlikely cry, 'You are Lobby Lud and I claim my five pounds.' But we knew that he was part of southern folklore and that he was employed by the *News Chronicle*.

But these promotions were part of a more innocent age —a time that, rumour has it, the *Daily Mirror* recently attempted to recreate as part of its admirable struggle to maintain standards and circulation simultaneously. It is said that, a short while ago, the plan was to give money away to anyone who was carrying a copy of the paper and accosted a reflective '*Mirror* man' with a demand to 'give us a big kiss'. There are conflicting explanations as to why the idea was abandoned. Some say that the pilot scheme revealed that no one dared make the passionate request, since the mistake an off-duty policeman or holidaying stevedore for the *Mirror's* travelling benefactor might result in immediate arrest or sudden unconsciousness rather than instant cash payment. Others claim that Sir Alex Jarratt, Chairman of Reed International and thus a *Mirror* supremo, was not prepared to take the responsibility for an epidemic of minor sexual assaults breaking out all over Britain.

Perhaps the stories are no more than the invention of the affectionate detractors who work for the *Mirror* with the confidence that enables them to ridicule it from time to time. There is, however, no doubt that one *Mirror* promotion enjoyed a brief — though hilarious — existence. Pound notes were planted at supermarkets and filling stations, and after they had been in circulation for a day or two, their noted numbers were published in the paper together with a promise of a substantial reward for any reader who found one. The initial response was a sensation — though not quite the sensation the *Mirror* had planned.

Banks phoned to complain that queues were building up at tellers' windows as customers carefully examined the number on each pound note they received. There were reports from London Transport of chaos at Tube stations as commuters examined their change with unusual care. Unfortunately most of the planted notes totally disappeared. In six weeks, the *Mirror* only received four successful claims and gave away only £25,000 of the £200,000 it had budgeted for prize money. Douglas Long, the Mirror Group's Chief Executive, hopes that the experience has taught the Government something about the money supply and the velocity of circulation. It taught him that there was no escape from bingo.

For the *Mirror*, as for its competitors, bingo has provided success of a sort. It is impossible to unravel the real reason for recent changes in circulation figures. And nobody is prepared to give the credit to 'legs eleven' and 'Maggie's den' alone. Bruce Matthews, Managing Director of Murdoch's News Group, at first seems unrepentant in his enthusiasm for the game that Rupert has played with undoubted commercial success on three continents. But he is cautious about its effect on News Group sales. The *Sun* is rising. The *News of the World* has halted its disastrous decline. But part of the *Sun's* success is the result of carefully manipulated cover prices. And the *News of the World* is temporarily buoyed up by the introduction of a colour magazine — a certain short-term boost to circulation. Both papers have benefited from softening their political line to reflect the views of readers rather than the prejudices of editors.

In fact, most of Fleet Street is embarrassed about bingo. Nobody really wants to claim that it is the reason why people buy their papers. Few frustrated executives have gone as far a Douglas Long who announced that he 'did not go into the newspaper business to become a bingo-caller'. And Jocelyn Stevens of Express Newspapers is reported to have described the game as 'the most dramatic and effective newspaper promotion there has ever been'. But the general attitude is apologetic and defensive. Every newspaper is publishing numbers because the others do it and refuse to stop. With *Mirror* and *Star* sales up by 300,000 and the *Sun* selling almost half-a-million extra copies it will be difficult to find a paper brave enough to break the vicious circle.

However, it remains an essentially demeaning business — pathetic from the point of view of journalists and readers alike. Bruce Matthews argues that it is really just another promotion, a natural successor to the largely ineffective £10 million that he spent on advertising last year. And in one commercial sense it is. But it also reflects the uncertainty of the whole industry — perhaps the whole nation. Twenty per cent of people who take News Group bingo cards are unemployed, grasping at an outside change of having money in their pockets again. And most of the people who buy an extra paper read only the numbers that it publishes to build up brief hopes as they pass their 12p across the newsagent's counter. We will know that the Depression has passed when newspapers are once more bought and sold because of their content.

Tiny Hands

WHEN DAVID ASTOR sold the *Observer* I was Secretary of State for Prices and Consumer Protection and, therefore, custodian of the Monopolies Act, a statute which contained specific and onerous clauses intending to avoid the concentration of newspapers in the hands of too few proprietors.

61

The law made no attempt to define the sort of people who are fit to become Press barons, and their commoner equivalents. All that mattered was how many titles the prospective buyer already possessed. And even if the predators owned more papers than Citizen Kane, the Act required their greater aggrandisement if the 'acquisition' provided the difference between closure and continued existence.

It was a time of continuous uncertainty. The *Standard* and the *Evening News* eyed each other across Fleet Street like gun-fighters anxious to draw but reluctant to shoot. The sun had begun to set on the Beaverbrook empire. And the fall of the House of Astor added a touch of class to the bids and the bargains. Most of the punters could have calculated on the back of a share coupon if they were eligible to pick up one of the pieces. But they all seemed to think that they had a ritual duty to visit my Department and describe their intentions.

Sir James Goldsmith came alone, smoked huge cigars, answered even the most technical questions without opening his briefcase, and explained that owning a paper was, for him, the way of fulfilling his longstanding political ambitions. I told Victor Matthews (then a commoner) that I would not stand between him and the two *Expresses* if he promised that his editorials would demand the return of Geoffrey Boycott to the England team. Civil servants from my Department were still trying to convince him that the cricket qualification was a joke when the *Observer* crisis broke. Pessimists said that collapse was inevitable. Then, on the south coast of California, God leapt out of a machine labelled 'Atlantic Richfield'.

At about the same time 'Tiny' Rowland's Lonrho company was in pursuit of SUITS, a Scottish concern with oblique newspaper interests. Technically, I ought to pigeon-hole Mr Rowland in my mind with the captains of industry who were anxious to buy other manufacturing companies — Lord Weinstock hard on the heels of Avery weighing machines, and Keith Showering in hot pursuit of Joe Lyons. But I think of Mr Rowland as a prospective newspaper tycoon, not least because whenever he came to see me he wanted to talk about his plans to improve the world. And he always seemed the sort of person who would prefer to propogate those views by buying a paper rather than by standing for election to his parish council and then hoping to become an MP in a decade or two. Whenever he entered my office he trailed clouds of contention and controversy behind him.

It was with mixed feelings that I discovered that he had bought the *Observer*. Ten per cent of the mixture was relief that a great Sunday paper had been saved from extinction. The rest was concern about what the *Observer* would become under Mr Rowland's ownership; an anxiety only partly relieved by the formal promise that its editorials would retain the right 'to comment on — and if necessary criticize — the affairs of Lonrho'. That phrase appeared in an *Observer* leader as recently as December 13th, in an issue that reawakened my fears about its relationship with its owner.

The integrity of Donald Trelford, the *Observer's* editor, is beyond question. And, since he commissioned my first freelance article (*Sheffield Telegraph* circa 1959, 'My Most Memorable Christmas', 3 guineas) his judgement must be of a similar high order. Indeed, the December 13th issue highlights the problem faced by an honest and able editor whose paper sails in financially rough water under the flag of a controversial and cost-conscious businessman, who would, for instance, be astonished if one of his loss-making employees refused a gift of £80,000.

That was the payment which the *Observer* received for publishing a bizarre eight-page diatribe financed by what its own Washington correspondent called 'a small, obscure, ultra-conservative group based in Brazil'. The advertising supplement ended with a reminder of 'the glorious future of France according to St Pius the Xth' whose gifts of prophesy confirmed the view that 'the socialist goals of France' include 'marriage put on the same basis as cohabitation, complete sexual freedom, and rehabilitation of homosexuality'.

Some *Observer* radicals insist that to refuse such an advertisement would itself be a denial of freedom and recall that long before Lonrho took charge the paper's pages carried an expensive attack on the Grunwick trade unions financed by the National Association for Freedom. It is, however, a strange freedom that requires a great paper to print eight pages of barely literate nonsense whenever cranks offer it money. The little disclaimer by the Washington correspondent only makes matters worse. It shows a wish to wound but a fear to refuse the cash.

But taking money from the Societies for Defence of Tradition, Family and Property was not the only cause for concern on unlucky Sunday the 13th. That morning the *Observer's* second leader was an attack on the Monopolies Commission for denying Mr Rowland (the creator of a 'massive and successful world-wide trading group') control of the House of Fraser. Did nobody at the meetings that decide such things argue that a paper owned by Mr Rowland is going to be read with constant apprehensive suspicion? Did nobody suggest that 'Tiny's' paper, like Caesar's wife, had to express unequivocally irreproachable opinions? Or did they simply wish that there was some way in which the law could define the sort of people who should be allowed to own newspapers?

Managing Editors

IT MAY WELL be that as you read this article — comfortably reflected in your breakfast table's silver, or perused from the leather embrace of a Pall Mall clubman's chair — Rupert Murdoch (proprietor of *The Times, Sunday Times, Sun, News of the World*, the nastiest paper in New York and sundry Antipodean publications) will be languishing in jail. It is even possible that Frank Giles, the *Sunday Times* Editor, will be with him in the exercise yard. Indeed, in these over-crowded days Gerald Long, Managing Director of Times Newspapers Limited, may join them in a single cell and they will all slop out together.

If these unhappy events come to pass, they will be the result of Mr Rupert Murdoch breaking the promises he made when he persuaded the Secretary of State for Trade to allow him to purchase *The Times* and *Sunday Times* without the Monopolies Commission investigating the desirability of such an acquisition. The Fair Trading Act 1973 is quite specific in prescribing prison sentences for 'persons knowingly concerned in' breaking conditions laid down by the Government when a newspaper merger is approved under section 58 of that Act. So, for a few days, one of Her Majesty's prisons can at least look forward to appointing a superior class of librarian. The job would go to Mr Giles. The other two defendants are not notably bookish.

The case for the prosecution is easily described. On January 27th the Secretary of State for Trade published the terms of the 'consent' by which he agreed to Murdoch buying *The Times* and *Sunday Times*. Item 4(b) (iv), again, is specific. 'The editor of each newspaper shall retain control over the appointment, disposition and dismissal of journalists.' In four instances — Ron Hall (out), Hugo Young (down), Brian MacArthur and Peter Jackson (in) — there is much evidence to suggest that the undertaking was ignored.

With the departure of Harry Evans to *The Times*, Frank Giles, his 63-year-old deputy and foreign editor, became the boss of Murdoch's one posh Sunday paper. Ron Hall (editor of the colour magazine) and Hugo Young (political editor) became joint seconds-in-command. Most of their colleagues agree that their primary duty was to support Giles during his caretaker years. Few people think that the triangular relationship succeeded. Indeed, it is generally agreed that failure was unavoidable.

Failure took the form of a simple deterioration in the paper. It became visibly duller and, in the jargon of the trade, looked 'old and tired'. Fears grew that the ten per cent fall in sales suffered by every quality Sunday paper would be recovered by the competition but not by the *Sunday Times*. Redemption seemed to lie in an improved magazine. So when Murdoch (more avenger than redeemer) made one of his brief and frantic visits to London, he sent for Ron Hall and made two specific complaints.

The *Observer* had 'got in first' with a food series. And the 'Look' feature (the women's section which it was planned to transfer to its own colour magazine) was not developing in the lively way the proprietor intended. Two days later, Hall was told by Giles that he was no longer deputy editor or boss of the colour supplement. Peter Jackson (late of *Drive, TV Times* and *Sunday*) was to take his place on the magazine. Brian MacArthur was to move from *The Times* to become joint deputy editor with Young. In reality, MacArthur displaced both his rivals. In Giles's absence the paper belongs to him.

The idea — promoted by the less than detached *Observer* — that all this came about as a result of a political conspiracy is pure fantasy. Paul Johnson (the hammer of radical journalists) did have lunch with Murdoch in early January, but neither the political inclinations of Hall and Young nor Johnson's powers of persuasion suggest that the meeting led to a pogrom. Murdoch simply wanted new men near the top. At a *Sunday Times* lunch on Friday January 15th Gerald Long observed that 'Change for change's sake is a good thing in newspapers. Rupert believes that and so do I.'

The changes may add some much-needed zip to a flaccid paper. MacArthur, in the words of File's announcement, became 'watchdog and encourager'. Jackson flew out to America immediately after his appointment to receive instructions from the boss. No doubt he had not had time to read paragraph 4(b) (iii) of the Consent: 'Instructions to journalists shall be given only by the editor or those to whom he has delegated authority.'

The conditions are equally specific about hiring and firing. Yet in his letter to *Sunday Times* journalists Frank Giles, a man of undisputed honour, did not even argue that the decision to replace Hall and Young with MacArthur and Jackson had been his. 'I, as editor, was involved in the discussion with higher management that led to these decisions.' When asked by the unions to decipher this coded message, he said that he had no wish to change the wording of his memorandum. Last week, when asked by me the same sort of question, he said, 'The decision was mine.' When pressed as to whether it had been initiated or endorsed by him, he declined to expand.

In his letter to the staff Giles insisted that he 'informed the people concerned in the changes as it was my right and duty to do'. But his rights and duties under the agreement between Murdoch and Government require him to preserve the freedom of his paper by genuinely taking decisions about appointments and dismissals. At one meeting with staff he said that he 'condoned' Murdoch's decision. I wonder if the Government will now do the same for him?

66

Tough Times

IF WE ASSUME that Rupert Murdoch is not stupid, we must conclude that he used his time and energy last week in a genuine bid to save *The Times* and *Sunday Times*. And since not even his bitterest critics have accused him of stupidity, we must discard the notion that the deperate days and dramatic nights were spent in devious determination to ensure that the negotiations collapsed, the papers closed and the journalists and printers formed neat queues outside their local Job centres. For such an outcome would have destroyed one of Mr Murdoch's potentially profitable assets. And it would have destroyed it for ever.

The idea that he was playing to lose has the enormous Fleet Street appeal of combining conspiracy with cataclysm. And the scenario does possess a superficial plausibility. First, the precious titles would be transferred from *Times Newspapers Limited* to *News International*, thus side-stepping the irksome restrictions on the management of the papers that Mr Murdoch accepted as the price of avoiding a Monopolies Commission enquiry. Then, the unions would be asked to accept impossible terms for the continuation of the papers in their present form. The rejection of the ultimatum would be the apparent cause of final closure.

But according to this canard, the locked doors and drawn curtains in Gray's Inn Road would be the interlude not the end. In a few months *The Times* and *Sunday Times* would arise from the dead and resume life free from the stifling embrace of the unions and the clammy hand of Government. The only problem about that devious plan is that it would not work. The Polaris commander who caused the holocaust would have to surface and invite cooperation from what was left of the world he had devastated. Even in the depths of a depression the newspaper unions do not forgive easily and the readers and advertisers forget all too quickly. Rupert Murdoch knows the penalties of closure.

There is, of course, no doubt that he was after blood. But he wanted to spill it at the carefully calculated speed of his choice. Thus, the first 'deadline' for the union's acceptance of six hundred redundancies was extended by twenty-four hours. At the end of the unsuccessful second day the announcement of 210 'compulsory redundancies' had the practical result of prolonging the period of last-ditch negotiation for another couple of weeks. Technically, the time was needed for the notices to take effect. Tactically, the extra fortnight provided a period in which the shock waves would subside and the unions would ponder the alternative to submission. By Tuesday Mr Murdoch was willing to withdraw the notices if 'sufficient volunteers for redundancy came forward'.

The technique was not simply to prolong and rule. The venerable principle of divide and rule was applied as well. 'We wish', Mr Murdoch said in his official statement, 'to record our thanks for the good will shown by many of the chapels (union branches) and their leaders. But sadly, we have had no sensible response from the others and in particular NATSOPA Clerical.' Mr Murdoch was gambling that if he picked on the clerical employees — telephonists, secretaries, messengers and the like — they would receive little support from other trade unions and might even be urged to accept reality by their own union executive.

As Rupert Murdoch sees it, reality is easily described. He wants to own a *Times* that does not lose more than a million pounds every month. Indeed, he wants to own a *Times* that makes a profit. For he is the newspaper proprietor as businessman not as propagandist, and every commercial fibre of his being is mortally offended by a 'profit centre' (or whatever he calls *The Times* in his subconscious) that rejects the opportunities provided by modern technology and insists on employing more staff than are essential to the economic needs of optimum output.

So he decided on a long war of attrition, knowing that the divided unions could only fight to save the jobs he chose to sacrifice by risking the massive redundancies of a total shutdown. NATSOPA seemed the most vulnerable union. With well over a thousand jobs involved on the *Sunday Times* colour supplement at the Sun Printers in Watford it was under especially strong pressure to keep the masthead flying. On the afternoon of 'deadline' Sunday the management thought the salami tactic had worked and that NATSOPA had agreed to slice off 350 of its members.

When, next day, the management discovered either its

error or NATSOPA's change of mind, it decided to complete the redundancy equation in its own way — 210 sackings plus forty unfilled vacancies plus eighty jobs lost by natural wastage equals the 330 reduction in staff that some NATSOPA officials seemed to swallow. Murdoch gambled on the opposition of local officials being overridden by the national executive or undermined by individual members willing to 'face the facts' and go quietly.

The National Union of Journalists were left unsure about what the facts really were. They believed that they had behaved with admirable responsibility — accepting the loss of fifty jobs a year ago, watching fifty new journalists join the paper during the last twelve months yet still agreeing to discuss the possibility of staff reductions. They, too, thought that they had struck a deal on the theoretically fateful Sunday. But the principle of a 'minimum staff level which the editor could not go below without negotiations' was questioned the day after it seemed to be agreed.

Negotiations conducted at gunpoint on the edge of an abyss are likely to end with the participants confused about what they proposed and what their protagonists accepted. Indeed, the extraordinary aspect of *The Times* crisis weekend is the calm way in which it ended. The paper came out on Tuesday. Mr Murdoch continued to make complimentary noises in the direction of the union leadership. Harry Evans popped up on radio to predict long life and happiness for the institution which he edits.

With the prospect of unemployment about to turn into reality for so many *Times* employees, no one could call the events of last week a phoney war. But it was certainly not the big battle. That will probably begin with the annual negotiation of new wage agreements and — unless Rupert Murdoch has badly miscalculated — will end with his victory over a weakened opponent and the sort of *Times* he always intended.

Rupert Bare

AS MY EXPERIENCE of internecine warfare is limited to the
Labour Party and the Yorkshire County Cricket Club, the
recent outbreak of fratricide at *The Times* newspaper seems,
to me, Byzantine beyond belief. The previous sentence did
not end with a cliche. For when, on crisis Sunday, I was told
that Mr Geoffrey Smith of that benighted paper had
appeared on radio and given a recital of extracts from other
people's confidential correspondence, I simply refused to
believe it. But it happened. Mr Smith read out parts of a
memorandum sent by his editor, Harold Evans, to his proprietor, Rupert Murdoch. The object of this revelation was to
prove that far from fighting for *The Time's* independence, his
beleaguered boss was perfectly prepared to ask for the
owner's instructions when it suited him to do so.

The 'Smith Affair' is tragically typical of what has
happened at *The Times*. Men and women, proud of their
discretion and certain of their integrity, have lost their heads
and their nerves and, in consequence, also mislaid important
parts of their reputation. To the naive outsider, it seems that
The Times can never be the same again. Even with Harry
Evans enjoying his unemployment in some Alpine resort and
his champion (ex-features editor, Anthony Holden) luxuriat-
ing in the aura of honourable resignation, it is only reasonable
to expect the bitterness to persist. But the Establishment's
great strength is its cohesive sense of self-preservation. The
upheavals were all intended to make it the Establishment's
paper again.

The argument that Mr Holden carried on as surrogate for
Harry Evans was in part true. Rupert Murdoch wanted a
'harder' political line in favour of President Reagan,
monetarism, and law and order. He also thought that Mr
Evans — who has grown trendier with the years — was far too
charitable towards the Social Democratic Party. Of course,
the policy positions which Mr Murdoch advocated were consistent with his own political prejudices. But he also believed
that a change of tone would enable *The Times* to take readers
from the *Daily Telegraph*. Harry Evans wanted to take on the
Daily Telegraph too. But he thought that his way of fighting
the circulation war was better than his proprietor's. With the

support of the paper's staff, Mr Evans's will would have prevailed. But he did not have it.

Last week at *The Times* anyone who had been employed in Printing House Square before Mr Evans's arrival last year was contemptuously called 'the old guard' by the middle-aged Turks that the new editor appointed. Not all the 'old guard' were old and many of them supported Harry Evans's continued editorship. But some of them were venerable in thought, word and deed. Their anonymous indictment of Mr Evans's brief reign was always expressed in *Times* patois. Before he came it had been 'primarily a serious paper . . . a paper of record . . . judging issues carefully and intellectually . . . consistent . . . committed to collegiate discussion'. After his arrival, 'the tone became confused . . . too many contrary currents . . . policies were changed by whim.'

The whims all belonged to Harry Evans. He was essentially an interfering editor, who read his colleagues' copy, sometimes sent it back for re-writing and — worst of all — arrived every morning with a head full of new ideas. Not even his friends say that the Evans style was easy to work with. And his friends grew fewer and fewer. For he made the crucial political mistake of introducing just the wrong number of new faces. Although he infuriated the established senior staff by negotiating four dozen redundancies and then appointing almost as many new journalists, he did not bring in enough allies to protect his position. He was essentially dependent on people who never wanted him.

When Rupert Murdoch began to put on the pressure there were too few people prepared to stand up for an editor whom his closest friends called 'quixotic' as a euphemism (for in *Times* journalists it could not be simple ignorance) for 'inconsistent'. And the pressure from Mr Murdoch became very strong. It was primarily concerned with the paper's massive weekly losses. But in Fleet Street — as Harry Evans said at the lunch where Granada Television made him Editor of the Year — independence and viability are indivisible. Rupert Murdoch never gave his editor an overall budget within which Evans could have worked and manoeuvred. As a result, the proprietor had to be consulted about detailed spending plans. Inevitably Murdoch used those favourable opportunities to talk about policy as well.

Which brings us back to the 'Smith Affair'. The letter from which Mr Smith quoted was said by him to reveal that Harry Evans's battle against Rupert Murdoch had nothing to do with editorial independence. For according to Mr Smith's interpretation of the document, the editor was already consulting the proprietor about policy. If Mr Smith thought such a revelation would reassure *Times* readers that their paper would have an independent life after Mr Evans's metaphorical death, he ought to improve his logic before he writes another leader. In any case the memorandum that Mr Smith leaked was full of technical questions about 'backset specials' and the *cost* of various ways of reporting the Budget.

I am not competent to judge if the letter was about policy, money, or both. What intrigues me are the questions concerning why Mr Smith chose to leak the letter and where he got it from. Theoretically a copy could have come from the new editor, Charlie Douglas-Home. But he denied complicity when cross-examined by the Press Association, and 'deprecated' the whole event. Indeed, all but Mr Evans's most passionate supporters insist that Mr Douglas-Home behaved throughout the whole affair as well as could be expected in an ambitious heir apparent, at one stage being quoted as saying that he would 'never edit a newspaper owned by that disruptive monster'.

The letter could have come from that disruptive monster's office. Or Mr Smith could have broken into the building late at night wearing a Dick Turpin mask, a black and white hooped jersey, armed with a jemmy and carrying a bag marked 'swag'. Nothing is past belief as far as the happenings at Printing House Square are concerned.

Sinking Feeling

THE STORY SO FAR. The Shrimsley Brothers (Bernie and Tony) are snatched from obscurity to edit a new paper — the *Mail on Sunday*. It is a flop. Roy Hattersley, boy journalist, reveals that the television critic is not John Osborne, the Conservative

MP for Sheffield Hallam, but an ageing playwright. Tony Shrimsley (the Hotspur of Fleet Street) defends the family honour with a full-page article attacking Roy Hattersley, boy politician. It proves Shrimsley's class as a popular journalist by ingeniously avoiding reference to any political event that took place after 1978. Hattersley's wrath is swift and terrible. Next day Bernard is sacked as *Mail on Sunday* editor. Tony picks up his cards the following week. *Now read on.*

The problem — at least for the *Mail on Sunday* — is that hardly anyone will respond to that stern injunction. Despite a unique front-page apology for its earlier inadequacies, the paper will go on losing money for years. As an indication of the state of desperation into which the management has fallen, the leader page is now occupied by attacks on rival papers. Last week, the *Mail on Sunday* trained its pop-gun on a target ripe for bombardment. Its wholly justified indictment of the *Daily Express* (reinforced with a splendid imitation of a vicious Cummings cartoon) can easily be set out.

No newspaper (not even the *Mail* itself) beat more loudly upon the patriotic drum during the Falklands campaign. Day after day, the *Daily Express* described the Task Force as a crusading army that could lead the entire nation into a new era of service and sacrifice.

'There is,' wrote Peter McKay (a man who leaves no cliche unturned), 'a silver lining to every cloud, even the black ones now scudding across the Falklands Sound.' And he had neither time nor respect for 'anyone who does not care and who treasures only their (sic) own comfortable life'.

Those moral degenerates, Mr McKay reminded us, 'can argue indefinitely against honour'. He went on like that day after day, excoriating the 'old failures — in spirit if not fortune — who stands (sic) always on the sidelines of life jeering' and who 'toy with lives in order to push their narrow interests'.

This column is concerned with neither the intellectual inadequacy of Mr McKay's arguments nor his incomplete command of the English language. His only importance is that together with Jean Rook ('So you thought the Land of Hope and Glory was asleep') he outdid the editorials in describing the Falklands campaign as a process of national regeneration in which we 'gave ourselves back some of the

73

weight and dignity we once had and many thought we had lost for good'.

I suspect that the paper's proprietor, Lord Matthews, felt his patriotic heart beat a little faster every time he read such stirring stuff. After all, one of his proudest boasts is that he is irresistibly attracted to great British institutions — the Ritz, the *Express,* the Cunard shipping line, all of which he bought for his Trafalgar House holding company.

Cunard actually went to war. The *Queen Elizabeth II* became a hospital ship. The *Atlantic Conveyor* carried stores and Harrier jets to replace those lost in the early days of the battle. Lord Matthews expressed his public admiration for the men who gave up their holidays and worked extra hours to refit the *QE2* for the South Atlantic adventure.'The dockyard workers have done wonders to get the ship ready on time,' he said, adding gratuitously, 'and if everybody else showed the same fantastic spirit we would not have any problems in this country.'

Alas, the 'fantastic spirit' which so moved Lord Matthews seems not to have suffused his whole empire. The *Atlantic Conveyor* lies at the bottom of the sea after which it was named, sunk by an Exocet missile which killed the captain and five of his crew. The replacement is not to be built in Britain (of which, according to its mast-head, Lord Matthews's *Express* claims to be the 'voice') but Korea or Japan. Peter McKay told us that the Falklands crisis 'helped us to assess things at home with more clarity'. It clearly helped the Cunard subsidiary of Trafalgar House to think more carefully about maximizing its profits. The more McKay talked of honour, the more they counted their return on capital.

The case for replacing the *Atlantic Conveyor* with a ship built in Japan or Korea must not go by default. Fortunately the case for Lord Matthews's defence was set out in a national newspaper — the *Daily Express*. Leith McGrandle, the Business Editor, explained that Lord Matthews 'has made clear that he would prefer to buy British . . . but for certain orders British shipbuilders cannot bring out the keenest prices'. Very clearly, if the decision to recapture the Falklands had been left to the Cunard directors, they would have decided not to waste the company's money on the reacquisition of a few barren acres. But then, as Mr McKay makes a point of reminding us, 'Anyone who does not care and who treasures only their (sic) own comfortable life can argue indefinitely against honour.'

On Friday, May 7th, Mr McKay drew our attention to the men who were 'heaving night and day in heavy seas'. Of course, he meant that the seas were heaving, not the men, but subsequent events must have made some of them want to vomit. Amongst the sailors who saw and heard their 'mates being blown to pieces' were the men of the *Atlantic Conveyor*. They returned home to discover that the flagship of P&O's fleet — also a veteran of the Falklands campaign — was to make 129 of their mates redundant. They are to be replaced by Indian seamen employed at about a quarter of their pay.

Apparently at Trafalgar House, Fleet Holdings, and the Cunard Company, such decisions can be reconciled with the crusader on the *Daily Express* mast-head, and the unashamed patriotism which is the paper's trademark. Perhaps there should be two mast-heads in future, or perhaps the Japanese will erect an extra flagstaff in the stern of the new *Atlantic Conveyor*. Then Trafalgar House could fly both of its double standards.

Three Legs Bad

TODAY WE BEGIN with a little textual analysis, comparing and contrasting two passages from contemporary journalism. Both concern the proposed merger of a mining company (Charter Consolidated) and a manufacturer of mining equipment (Anderson Strathclyde). Each deals, in particular, with the Monopolies Commission's formal judgement that the merger should be prohibited, the Government's decision to overrule that recommendation and the role in the affair of Lord Cockfield, the Secretary of State for Trade.

On December 22nd 1982, David Simpson and Julia Langdon, writing in the *Guardian,* reported that a junior Minister, Peter Rees, 'took over the responsibility from the

Trade Secretary on whether or not to accept the monopolies verdict because Lord Cockfield owns 2500 shares — worth £5,600 — in Charter.' Six days later, the *Isle of Man Weekly Times* told its readers that because Lord Cockfield owned '2500 shares — worth £5,600 — in Charter . . . Mr Rees took over the responsibility from the Trade Secretary on whether to accept the monopolies verdict.'

Perceptive students will notice the similarity in the two quotations, and will suspect that the Isle of Man story was copied from the national paper — a common and generally accepted practice in local journalism. The suspicion will be reinforced by the identical misuse of the preposition 'on' in place of the correct 'about', and the common valuation of Lord Cockfield's holding at £5,600 when other papers put the figure at £5,575. But the important point about the two stories is not their similarities but their one dramatic difference. Bill Dale, the editor of the *Isle of Man Weekly Times* and author of that paper's Cockfield story, was sacked because of its publication. As far as I can discover, no one at the *Guardian* has been dismissed for reporting the Trade Secretary's dilemma. But then the *Guardian* is not owned by one of Lord Cockfield's friends.

It must in fairness be said that Henri Dor, the owner of the *Isle of Man Weekly Times,* the *Manx Star,* the *Isle of Man Examiner* and *Manx Life,* insists that Mr Dale was not sacked as editor because of the Monopolies story alone. According to the owner, his employee of twelve years' standing had an unfortunate enthusiasm for sensationalism. It was demonstrated by his treatment of what the proprietor calls 'the rape case'. Indeed, Henri Dor told me that the account of that particular trial (accurately described in the paper as 'indecent assault', not 'rape') resulted in the unhappy editor being 'censured by the Tynwald'. Mr Dor then amended the record to 'censured *in* the Tynwald'. Robert Quayle, the Clerk to the Manx Parliament, told me, 'I cannot recall or find in my files any record of a formal complaint.' The Tynwald was in recess when the trial in question took place.

I have, of course, quoted only a small part of the editor/reporter's alleged attempt at sensationalism which appeared as the second lead on page three of his paper. The sensation with which he chose to dominate the front page was the building of a new motor-cycle track. Page two drove the readers wild with a story about whooping-cough. His account of the Cockfield incident — the Opposition's criticism and the Prime Minister's defence — was, in my view, at least as balanced as the stories in the national dailies. However, the proprietor has a second criticism to make. As well as choosing 'to quote the critics without publishing the other side of the story', Dale 'published an article about someone without contacting that person'.

Fleet Street might be a better place if all proprietors always insisted that employees on their papers published a piece about a politician only after giving the subject of the story an opportunity to defend himself. But if those who broke that golden rule were always sacked, a number of very distinguished by-lines would disappear from our breakfast-tables. In any case, reading Mr Dale's rehash of what had already been written elsewhere, few people would think that any defence was needed.

Lord Cockfield's own complaint is less about the content of the story than about the fact that the story appeared at all. He says (though Mr Dale denies it) that during a telephone conversation which followed publication, the offending journalist admitted that the article was 'biased and unfair'. But to Cockfield the real offence was the intrusion into what the *Sunday Telegraph* quoted him as calling 'a protected degree of anonymity'. The Secretary of State for Trade believes that as the Isle of Man is outside the jurisdiction of the British Parliament, he should be allowed to take refuge in his sea-shore bungalow whenever he feels like it without his ministerial activities being recorded by the local Press.

The idea that a news blackout might be imposed on the Isle of Man is, of course, bizarre — though not quite so preposterous as the notion that Lord Cockfield needs his anonymity protecting. Amongst the stories that have not appeared in Manx papers are accounts of the shirt being torn from his noble back by teenaged girls, riots outside his Ministry by the southern branches of his fan clubs, insatiate demands for locks of hair and constant pestering for autographs by Japanese tourists. Bill Dale has been sacked for reasons which are either squalid or absurd.

I hasten to add that Lord Cockfield himself neither

demanded nor suggested that Bill Dale be sacked. According to island gossip, he dined with proprietor Henri Dor the night before the editor was dismissed, and again on the day that Dale was told by his employer that if he 'grovelled' he might be reinstated. But Lord Cockfield (who not un-reasonably refuses to discuss his Christmas social engagements) is not the man to demean himself with such matters. Dor may have acted in his friend's interest, but not on his instruction. However, one thing (apart from the NUJ) could save Bill Dale from unemployment or re-engagement as a reporter on a twenty-five per cent wage cut. That is the intercession of Lord Cockfield. When I spoke to him, he was not prepared to demean himself in that way either.

Private Grief

Mother of Invention

THREE WEEKS AGO Joan Collins was the principal guest on Michael Parkinson's television programme. The mutton-chop sleeves of her little black dress were cut with such dramatic extravagance that she seemed encased in the sort of shoulder pads usually only associated with American football players. And her conversation was as bizarre as her appearance.

One of her stories concerned the occupational hazards which she faced whilst filming Cinzano advertisements. According to Miss Collins, actors in alcohol commercials are required — at least in front of the cameras — to drink the actual product they promote. Sipping visually identical, but innocuous, alternative liquids is, she assured us, against the law.

The Independent Broadcasting Authority's confirmation that no such rule exists increased my interest in the rest of Miss Collins's performance. I was particularly intrigued by her assertion that a book she had written — describing her daughter's recovery from a near fatal accident — would produce only 'minuscule profits'. Surely, I thought, some newspaper would pay five figures for the serial rights.

I assumed that paper to be the *Sun*. For on February 1st its front page boasted a 'world exclusive'. It was called 'Katy, how I saved my daughter's life'. Inside there was a three-page account of 'How I saved my little girl's life', liberally illustrated by pictures which I assumed to come from the Collins family album. The origin of the pictures may become a crucial issue if, as Miss Collins threatens, the *Sun* is sued for publishing the account of her 'little miracle' and the way she brought the supernatural event about by performing 'the hardest role I have ever played'.

The account of how 'you can will a person to get better' appeared under the by-lines of Lee Bury (in Los Angeles) and Sue Freeman. I first thought that they had been recruited to precis Miss Collins's magnum opus. Certainly, they were not employed to improve the literary quality of the story. 'It is just over eighteen months since Katy's accident,' the saga began, 'she is absolutely fantastic.'

On 'day two of the incredible Joan Collins story' both the

81

Sun and its subject exposed the professional rather than the private life of 'the biggest bitch on American television at the moment'. Of course, 'it upsets' the actress if people believe that the mother is really 'like that'. But she struggles on, conscious that she is 'still a sex symbol after thirty years in showbusiness' and aware of 'how precious and how short life is.'

Optimistic as always, I sensed a valediction in that final piety and hoped that it marked the point at which Katy would be left in obscurity to complete her convalescence. For I confess that I am not one of Miss Collins's warmest fans. I recall reading her 'story' in another newspaper years ago. It contained an account of how she lost her virginity. Since then I have suspected that she lacked reticence.

However, Katy, brought back from the dead, still cannot rest in peace. On February 14th the *Sunday Mirror* announced that 'angry Joan Collins hits back'. My judgement about her reticence factor was indicated. As well as asking the question 'Why have they hurt my Katy like this?' she told Eve Pollard about the trial separation from husband Ron, the lawsuit against ex-husband Tony and the problems of being a 'celebrity'.

One of them appears to be the risk of exploitation by newspapers. For 'Plans have been ruined for the serialization of her book based on her diaries she kept while Katy was fighting for survival.' It 'attracted the attention of a few newspapers . . . one of them sent a reporter to see me, supposedly to talk about my thirty years in showbusiness.' The result, according to Miss Collins, was an article about her daughter which looked 'like the authorized story' and ruined all prospect of some other daily paying the £40,000 for serial rights that the authoress is said to be asking.

Presumably it was the *Sun* that Miss Collins had in mind. If so, there is some dispute between her and Kevin McKenzie, the offending paper's editor, about whether or not she is suing the paper that 'deprived my nine-year-old daughter and children who could well do with the money'. According to the *Sunday Mirror*, she is. According to Mr McKenzie she is not — and he does not behave like a penitent preparing for an apologetic appearance in the dock.

Mr McKenzie insists that his reporters visited Miss

Collins for 'an interview about *Dynasty,* a soap opera in which she plays' (in the words of the *Sun* interview) a 'mean and nasty female J. R. Ewing'. Miss Collins talked 'obsessively' about her daughter and the reporter found the child a more interesting subject than the television series. Whatever else is disputed, Miss Collins will not deny the existence of the obsession. In the *Sunday Mirror's* unequivocally sympathetic article, Eve Pollard is precise about the subject, 'Katy has become an obsession with Joan, she admits it.'

What many readers of the rival papers will find difficult to understand is the reason why the tabloids of their choice wrangle over the bodies of the recently recovered Katy Collins and her incredibly well-preserved mother. Admittedly, Miss Collins has acquired a place in British folklore similar to that enjoyed in modern Egyptian culture by the monuments at Abu Simbel — miracles of conservation, triumphs for the restorer's art, proof that the harder the surface the less the erosion. But there is more to it than that.

Joan Collins combines qualities that are individually attractive for popular papers and which, added together, are irresistible to the lower end of the Fleet Street market. She is maternity in a *Merry Widow* corset, pulchritude in black stockings and suspender belt. She hovers between the opulence of Sunset Boulevard and the hard reality of family responsibilities. She is the middle-aged lady who has defeated middle age. Miss Collins is whatever fantasy we care to make from her. A meaningless myth is a precious property for any paper.

Street Price

I TELEPHONED THE *Sun* several times last week. I offer as an excuse for my deviant behaviour an interest that I had developed in a multiple story which the paper had printed on November 3rd. On that day a triptych of tragedy was spread across pages sixteen and seventeen. Under its headline — 'The Hell of Having a Drug Addict Son' — readers were told 'Three famous fathers talk about the tragedy drugs brought into their lives.' What readers were carefully not told was whom the fathers actually talked to.

The three famous fathers were Joss Ackland (actor), Colin Tennant (Socialite) and David Kossoff (entertainer). Mr Tennant was pictured with his 'son Charlie who became hooked on heroin'. According to the story (subtitled 'fussing made it worse') young Mr Tennant is now well on his way to recovery and rehabilitation. Joss Ackland's son Paul and Paul Kossoff, son of David, are both dead. Paul Ackland died on October 7th.

Joss Ackland published a notice of his son's death in the *Times* obituary columns. Inevitably, the carrion descended upon him and his grief. First there was a 'young boy' from an agency who stood outside the Ackland house 'in the pouring rain'. He was eventually persuaded to leave with the promise that, looking back on years of doorstepping, abandoning the story 'might be the one thing in life that he could be really proud of'. Then, whilst Mr Ackland was in France visiting his student daughter, the Coroner's office sent him a message. The newspapers had discovered the date of the inquest. He should expect 'to be besieged'.

It was the thought of the siege that persuaded Mr Ackland, a journalist's son, to take pre-emptive action. As he dwelt in the public domain, some account of his son's death was unavoidable. But if a paper could be persuaded to treat it with sensitivity and dignity, the scandalmongers might lose interest. In any event, having spoken to a decent journalist, he could refuse to talk to the foot-in-the-door brigade. He phoned two editors — Peter Preston of the *Guardian* and Donald Trelford of the *Observer*. Both agreed to send journalists to see him. Mr Ackland insisted that both should come at the same time, He had no intention of telling the same harrowing tale twice.

Mr Ackland is, of course, open to two charges. The first is that he attempted to manipulate the news. That seems to me a charge barely worth making — particularly if it comes from those editors who pay undesirables to keep their sordid stories exclusive to one particular paper. In any event, a grieving father is entitled to protect his family from Fleet Street's intrusion. Decent people must regret that the stratagem failed.

The second charge is more serious. If Mr Ackland had not been President Peron, was not Falstaff and about to become Captain Hook, he probably would have been unable to speak either to Trelford or Preston. Undoubtedly he was taking advantage of his fame and reputation. But had it not been for that fame and reputation, the gutter press would not have been in hot pursuit. Compassionate people will argue that since it was his famous name that titillated the worse tabloids, he was entitled to use it in protection of his family against those papers' gross excesses.

The *Guardian* published its story on October 30th. The *Observer's* virtually identical version appeared the following day. 'At no time in his life,' Mr Ackland insisted, was his son 'a drug addict'. He hoped that the family could mourn in peace. However, on the morning of November 3rd he was approached by the London Broadcasting Company with a request for him to take part in a serious programme on drug abuse. He declined, saying that despite his wish to warn others, he was determined not to prolong the agony beyond the single *Guardian/Observer* interview. 'What about the article in today's *Sun?*' the producer asked him.

The article in the *Sun* was a literal pastiche, the *Guardian* and *Observer* interviews cut up into pieces and re-arranged in a way that made it look as if Mr Ackland had actually been interviewed by that paper. The impression that the story legitimately belonged to the *Sun* ('three famous fathers talk . . .') was heightened by the inclusion of a by-line. The author was said to be one Lee Rodwell. No one took the blame for the Tennant and Kossoff stories which were also included within the same 'Drug Addict Son' headline, a description which Ackland specifically rejected.

I thought therefore that it might be interesting to find out if any one of the trio had actually talked directly to the *Sun*. Unable to find Mr Tennant's telephone number, my secretary asked Miss Rodwell (presumably a recent contact) where he could be found. When the promised information was not provided, I phoned the lady myself. Had she, I asked her directly, even talked to Mr Tennant? That, she said, is a question you must ask the Features Editor. The phone went dead.

I phoned back and the Executive Features Editor herself,

Wendy Henry, was on Miss Rodwell's line. Had I, she asked, any evidence to prove that the *Sun* had not spoken to Mr Tennant — a riposte which linguistic philosophers amongst the *Sun's* readers will not regard as an adequate answer to my question. Then Ms Henry warmed to her theme.

'I was,' she said, 'on the original story when it was in *Woman* magazine.' Enquiries about direct contact between Mr Tennant and the *Sun* were greeted with long silences, objections to 'silly questions' and, eventually, the assurance that 'I can vouch that he said every word of it.'

Perhaps the *Sun* did interview Mr Tennant, though I doubt it. They certainly never spoke to Joss Ackland. All they did was steal somebody else's copy. The episode is made both more poignant and more repulsive by the nature of the story which they stole. But this column is about newspapers, not morality. I therefore simply draw attention to the fact. When you read the *Sun* you can never be sure if it has anything new to say or if it is serving up some other paper's warmed-up left-overs.

Last Exits

THE WESTMINSTER CAREERS of two long-serving Members of Parliament came to an abrupt and spectacular end early in March 1982.

The Right Honourable Fred Mulley (Labour) was in the words of the *Guardian*, 'sacked by his Sheffield (Park) Constituency Party'. On the same day *The Times* announced that Sir Ronald Bell (Conservative) had 'died in his office at the Commons'. I confess bias about them both. Fred Mulley is my oldest friend in Parliament. I met him when I was still a student and, twenty years ago, he helped me to become the Parliamentary candidate for Sparkbrook. He was still helping me when we sat side by side in the Callaghan Cabinet. On the other hand, Sir Ronald Bell never even made a speech with which I remotely agreed. However, when I compare the newspaper coverage of their passing, it is on Sir Ronald's behalf that I feel a concern that borders on outrage.

Fred Mulley, 'ousted by Euro MP', was essentially a political story that demanded political treatment. As *The Times* correctly reported, the 'rejection' of a recent Cabinet Minister and Party Chairman by his constituency activists was 'a measure of Labour grass-roots militancy' in South Yorkshire. Editorials, like the *Guardian's* 'Mr Mulley Bites the Dust' were, no doubt, painful to the vanquished potential candidate. But they were legitimate comment on the state of the Labour Party. Sir Ronald, however, died of a heart attack, not political assassination. After thirty years on the shabby green benches, his end justified personal —perhaps even compassionate — reporting. That is not what it got.

The Times published a fourteen-column inch obituary, but its news story began 'A Social Democrat/Liberal Alliance by-election victory now threatens . . . ' The *Guardian* showed more respect for the proprieties and printed a shorter formal tribute but produced a news story that actually concerned Sir Ronald rather than his potential successors. The *Daily Express* — whose favourite campaigns Sir Ronald had fought from the Common Market through immigration control to Law and Order — produced three paragraphs. Two of them concerned the inconvenience his death would cause local Liberals. The third gave the size of the majority that the Liberal candidate would have to overcome. The *Daily Telegraph* behaved in much the same way. The announcement of the death of a Member of Parliament who had consistently supported *Daily Telegraph* causes was headed 'By-election in "Safe" Tory Seat'.

The *Financial Times* managed to fit in ten biographical lines at the end of nine inches of political analysis, headed 'Liberals Likely to Fight Bell Seat'. Eleanor Goodman's breathless commentary about which segment of the middle ground would lay claim to the Beaconsfield inheritance contained the reassuring news that 'No formal decision will be taken about which Alliance party will fight the seat until after Sir Ronald's funeral.' But that did not prevent her from speculating about the problems that contenders for the legacy would face. Miss Goodman was much concerned with the size of swing. 'Even with one a big as Mrs Shirley Williams got in Crosby, the Alliance would not be home and dry in Beaconsfield.' No figures were supplied. So it was impossible to compare literacy and numeracy.

Sir Ronald died on a Saturday afternoon and therefore received a brief mention in Sunday's papers before he was engulfed by political speculation the following day. Sir Thomas Galbraith, the Conservative Member for Glasgow Hillhead was unlucky enough to breathe his last after Sunday's papers had gone to press. So the fact of his death and its consequences were left for revelation and comment on Monday. 'Speculation was rife last night,' shouted the *Scotsman*, 'that Mr Roy Jenkins ... would contest the election which will have to be held in Glasgow.' The banner headlines on the front of the Scottish edition of the *Daily Mail* clearly rejoiced in the thought of 'Roy Caught in Allies' Haggle'. The *Glasgow Herald* actually put the 'death of Sir Thomas' in heavy type — as an explanation of why the SDP would 'send for Roy Jenkins'.

South of the Border, there was less hysteria but equally little respect. In the *Daily Telegraph*, where passion is always suppressed, Erica Rowe — the topless Twickenham streaker — shared the front page with 'Tory's Death Gives Chance to Jenkins'. Suburban sensibilities were respected by Miss Rowe appearing fully clothed and Sir Thomas being described by the affectionate diminutive 'Tam'. But the lead story was essentially about Roy Jenkins, 'the only member of the SDP's founding gang of four without a parliamentary seat'. The *Guardian* announced 'Hillhead By-election Problem for Torn Alliance'. The other problem — Galbraith's death — occupied the five lines necessary to explain the SDP/Liberal dilemma.

According to the *Guardian* the by-election became 'necessary because of the death on Saturday of Sir Thomas Galbraith'. *The Times* described the doleful occasion as happening on 'Saturday, two days after he was knighted'. On the other hand, Monday's *Scotsman* attributed the Hillhead contest to the sitting member's 'death yesterday'. So did Monday's *Glasgow Herald*. James Wrightman, in the *Telegraph*, voted for Sunday too. The truth is that some of them did not know the day of the death and none of them really cared. Thomas Galbraith's death was not the story. After more than thirty-five years in the House of Commons 'Scotland's longest serving Tory MP' performed his last duty to political journalists. He made an exciting by-election possible.

I do not suggest for a moment that Members of Parliament should be treated more tenderly than other mortals, either in life or after death. Indeed, I know to my cost that they are likely to be treated with a good deal less tolerance and understanding than are the members of other trades and professions. I accept and welcome the MP's special vulnerability. I have little time for the trappings of death or the rituals of mortality. But my distaste for the formalities of mourning are not shared, at least in public, by British newspapers. They are all for pious respect and what Rupert Brooke called 'duty by the dead' — unless, of course, such obligations stand in the way of a good story about a fashionable subject.

A Touch of the Sun

I HAVE SUSPECTED for some time that the *Sun's* public passion for Margaret Thatcher is not totally reciprocated (even in private) by the object of its proclaimed affection. True, Larry Lamb — the editor during the most purple period of sycophancy — left for the Australian Outback with a knighthood. But I do not believe that is is the paper to which the Prime Minister immediately turns when the bundle of next day's news arrives at Downing Street. In the old days above the shop in Grantham, it was undoubtedly the *Daily Express* that formed young Margaret's opinions. Now that (spiritually at least) she has moved to the outer suburbs, her choice must be the *Mail*. I sometimes think that she models her several moods on the published persons of *Mail* writers — Lynda Lee-Potter when she visits hospitals and homes for the elderly, and Ann Leslie when she excoriates her enemies.

But just as Parliament was rising for the summer recess, it was the *Express* which filled its front page with a picture of the Prime Minister (leaning uneasily forward in her chair as if caught in the act of changing from Lynda Lee-Potter to Ann

Leslie) and a heavily edited conversation between Margaret Thatcher and George Gale. The evidence of heavy editing is overwhelming. In the published 'interview of the year' Mrs Thatcher was allowed to speak for long periods without interruption or requests for refreshment. No one who knows Mr Gale believes him capable of such self-effacement.

The following day Mrs Thatcher spread her favours more recklessly. 'Maggie's Fury at Runcie's Sermon' and 'Maggie Angry Over Service' were heaven sent (if not heaven approved) headlines for the popular dailies. Attacking the Archbishop of Canterbury over the content of his sermon at the Falklands Thanksgiving service clearly gave the down-market tabloids the sort of pleasure enjoyed by little boys with catapults when they take aim against fat ladies caught in the act of tying their shoe-laces. But if the front pages were pure Bateman, inside were pictorial views of England, home and beauty.

For on the day that she was reported to be 'spitting blood' at 'pacifists and cringing clergy', the Prime Minister also addressed the National Union of Townswomen's Guilds. According to page two of the *Sun*, Mrs Thatcher 'blasted Britain's permissive society'. When the paper was closed, the fearless expose of the 'free love threat to Britain' rubbed against a page three pin-up representing Mary Queen of Scots. Jane Warner (to whom the tragic queen 'has always been a heroine') wore a wimple, a ruff, and nothing else.

The *Sun* did, of course, pioneer the breast as a major feature of British journalism. I suppose there was a time in the early Sixties when the sight of some taped-up young lady retained the power to excite. Now, the best thing that can be claimed for page three is the comfort of familiarity. The same circus of pneumatic girls rotated in a monthly cycle and decorated with increasingly obscure accoutrements to justify the silly caption that accompanies the picture, has pro-gressed from being the most daringly controversial to the most boringly predictable aspect of British journalism.

I do not suggest that the *Sun's* mammalian obsession is in any way inconsistent with the general support for family life and formal respectability. Indeed, in the same issue that reported Mrs Thatcher's attack on 'self-appointed experts who encourage children to grow up faster' it clearly gave its yellow seal of approval to self-appointed 'avenger James Arands who beat up a child-molester'. Arands, the *Sun* explained with righteous satisfaction 'returned home . . . to a hero's welcome' after being released from jail as the result of a 'massive mercy campaign'. Mr Arands (dissatisfied with the sentence imposed by the courts) had attacked a child-molester with a hammer, only to be convicted of assault and sentenced to eighteen months in jail by an ungrateful court.

James Arands achieved immortality in the pages of the *Sun* because he was let out. Fame came to 'fashion model Debra Keggler' in the same edition because an Old Bailey jury decided that she had never been locked up. Under the old-world headline 'Model Loses Lust Slave Plea', *Sun* readers discovered that her 'amazing allegations of a five-hour sex ordeal' had not impressed the court. Indeed, it concluded that 'the raven-haired beauty — who uses the name Amber in her work — was a willing partner in a passionate bedroom romp'.

You may laugh or you may sneer, but for sentimentalists like me, that story evokes the most poignant memories of lost youth. For a moment, I was back at the Wadsley Church Bible-class looking for the rude bits in the *Sunday Empire News*.

It was the headline that rolled the years away. It is, in its cheap way, a wonderful example of how maximum meaning can be compressed into minimum space. Three of its five words ('Model', 'Lust' and 'Slave') combined to heighten the sleazy interest. And it seems that the *Sun* can produce such journalistic gems at will. 'Council Love Nest for Vicar' (in the same edition as Debra Keggler's moment of glory) only scores one titillatory point in five words. But link such emotive words as 'vicar' and 'council' with 'love nest', and *Sun* readers believe that their fifteen pence have not been spent in vain.

Who are the people who produce such headlines? And how do they manage to keep up the standard day after day? 'Sex Taunts Led Ten-Pint Lover to Murder', they proclaimed last Wednesday, and followed it up (in case you think they never can recapture the first fine careless rapture) with 'Cage Me said a Fiend'. Are they old men with celluloid cuffs and stiff collars who reminisce about the time when they met Hannen Swaffer in El Vino's? Or are they young thrusters with gold bracelets who dream of becoming gossip columnists when they grow up? And to what occupation do they lay claim on the front page of their passports?

Cardinal Sin

THE DOG WHICH failed to bark is probably journalism's most hackneyed image. It concerns the importance of the unexpected, the implication of individuals and institutions not behaving in the way the unthinking and the uninformed anticipate. The significance of canine negligence was first observed by Sherlock Holmes on behalf of Conan Doyle. The theme was then developed by a fictional Catholic priest who had been created by a Catholic essayist and novelist. I have no doubt that G. K. Chesterton was a regular reader of the *Tablet*. Father Brown, being less of a conscious intellectual, undoubtedly read the *Catholic Herald*. As St Francis would understand, I mean no disrespect to either periodical when I say that neither of them barked last week. Malcolm Muggeridge was received into the Roman Catholic Church without either paper making a sound.

The posh Sundays splashed the glad news across their front pages and illustrated their accounts of the baptism with bespoke photographs. Ian Cook recorded 'Mr Malcolm Muggeridge kneeling' for the *Sunday Telegraph*. Both the Bishop of Arundel and Brighton and Lord Longford were pictured laying on hands in a perfectly arranged composition. Jane Brown in the *Observer* gave readers 'Malcolm Muggeridge is blessed'. In the *Sunday Times*, he was depicted eyes tight in meditation, almost totally obscuring the camera's view of Lord Longford. No doubt he will make amends for that sin against public relations at his next confession.

As far as I can make out, John Capon (Churches Correspondent of the *Sunday Telegraph*), Hugo Davenport of the *Observer*, and Alison Miller of the *Sunday Times* were actually there beside the font describing the way the Muggeridges 'folded away their spectacles' during the silence for prayer and recording Mr Muggeridge's aside concerning the way in which he had been 'mysteriously held back' from following the path to Rome before. Mr Hugo Davenport of the *Observer* put an end to the uncertainty of anyone who thought that the whole exercise might be in dubious taste. He began his story with a metaphor concerning the 'long dalliance with Rome', ending when Mr Muggeridge 'made the liaison official'.

Charity being more important than either faith or hope, I am prepared to give Mr Muggeridge the benefit of the doubt and believe that he was properly embarrassed by the publicity surrounding his Reception into the Roman Catholic church. Kneeling in the chapel 'at the bottom of Lord Longford's garden' he must have been reminded of Rex Mottram's baptism as recorded by Evelyn Waugh in *Brideshead Revisited.* Rex was so anxious to do the thing in style that he tried to arrange for a full supporting cast of Cardinals to be flown in from Rome. And he embraced his new faith with such uncritical certainty that he had invincible answers to all questions concerning dogma. Asked if he could reconcile the doctrine of Papal infallibility with a Pope insisting that it was raining on a cloudless day, Mr Mottram did not hesitate. It would, he explained, be raining spiritually. But some people would not be holy enough to see it. Yet despite such mountain-moving faith, Rex did not get onto the front pages of the Sunday papers.

But Rex was not part of Fleet Street's inbred obsession with itself and with its own. And Malcolm Muggeridge is the media man *par excellence.* He has worked for the *Guardian,* the *Daily Telegraph* and the *New Statesman.* He has edited *Punch* and he has pontificated on a thousand television programmes. He catholicly preceded his Catholicism by more than a decade. Ten years before what Hugo Davenport called his 'Romecoming', he could boast Lord Longford as a friend and Richard Ingrams, the editor of *Private Eye,* as a disciple. With a spectrum of new establishment friends which stretches all the way from the sacred to the profane, he is bound to be constantly in Fleet Street's mind. I suspect that on the night of Saturday November 27th 1982, news editors really did believe that the world was waiting for the latest word from the Chapel of Our Lady, Help of Christians, at Hurst Green.

In fact I have begun increasingly to suspect that the posh Sundays can be divided into two distinct parts — not colour magazines, reviews, arts sections and real newspapers; but the pages that are written for the general readership as distinct from the pages that are put together because they are of interest to a little coterie of metropolitan journalists. The 'review fronts' of the *Observer* and *Sunday Times* perfectly demonstrated the dichotomy.

The Observer began the month with 'It was Mrs Thatcher's War' by Max Hastings and Simon Jenkins, a genuinely fascinating account of the Falklands Campaign. It then turned to the Venetia Stanley correspondence, and reproduced a whole series of inconsequential letters from an ageing Prime Minister to a young lady of no intrinsic interest. None of them was written within the last sixty years. The *Sunday Times* changed with the approach of December. On November 7th and 14th its review front was devoted to 'Life in Happy Valley', a story of 'aristocrats, alcohol and adultery', concerning Josslyn Hay who was ' "asked to leave" Eton — where he was the object of intense schoolboy adoration — in 1918'. Then it ran two features of regrettably universal interest. They were called 'A Nation on the Fiddle'.

Of course, a weekend newspaper ought to find space for articles which are of interest because of the way in which they are written rather than the news that they carry. But in the *Observer* and the *Sunday Times,* there is always at least the implication that the subjects of the essays are as important as the style.

I get the feeling that readers are supposed to find Venetia Stanley and Josslyn Hay interesting in themselves. I, at least, cannot oblige. Nor can I understand the apparent importance of Mr Muggeridge's baptism. That essentially private event was treated properly in the Catholic weeklies. It was a matter of no theological importance and should have been left to gossip columns.

Gang Show

THE *SUNDAY PEOPLE* has changed. Under the control of its new editor, Nick Lloyd — and under the influence of his wife, Eve Pollard — is has not so much moved down-market as reduced its age. It now aims at not quite trendy teenagers and the young married couples which they become. But its increased interest in sex maintains some of the old innocence ('the rookie police girl and her roving Casanova') and occasionally 'The Voice of the People' thunders an editorial opinion that reflects an understanding of working-class respectability of which 'the paper for all the family' would have been proud. Last week its pronouncement on a major media event was couched in the language of a bishop reproving a vicar for an offence against canon law. 'It would,' its leader ran, 'have been more fitting if Mrs Kray had been given a quiet, decent burial.'

The Kray funeral was previewed on both radio and television. Jan Leeming was particularly poignant in her declaration that the twins (called by the *Sunday People* 'two of the most savage gangsters of the century') hoped for a decent send-off. Brother Charlie reinforced the news item with an interview in which he defined decency in the special context of his mother's burial. The family wanted a little quiet dignity. After the publicity build-up, there was not the slightest chance of their getting it.

The *Sun*, of course, behaved like the *Sun* — that is to say, deplorably. Its entire front page was devoted to a story which was sentimental ('last farewell to old mum') and sanctimonious ('the mother they did not deserve') in turn. Naturally, the *Sun* had a picture of Diana Dors 'paying homage'. Later in the week, the *Guardian's* much improved diary column suggested that her presence was not unconnected with her hope of playing 'the mother they did not deserve' in a film. Despite the Mafia-style dark glasses that she wore at the funeral, Miss Dors is not my choice for the part. If the *Sun's* picture is to be believed, Violet Kray might easily have been president of the Hoxton branch of the Irene Handl Look-alike Society.

Diana Dors could not, of course, have been one of 'the fading celebrities' whose graveside presence the *People* so deplored. For only a month ago she was still sufficiently celebrated to command that paper's front page with an article about her medical condition. Nor am I altogether clear about the identity of the 'simpering obituarists' to whom the *People* took equal exception. The real Fleet Street offence, to which the *People* was right to draw angry attention, was not the mawkish paragraphs written about 'the woman whose life had been made a misery by the evil sons she doted on' but the whole pages of coverage given to the attendance at her funeral of 'two men who were Britain's most notorious gangsters'.

In the *Daily Telegraph*, James Allan wrote of the 'simple solemnity of the occasion' in an article that monopolized all of page three except for one half-column-inch that announced the exhibition of a Roman mosaic floor in the Corinium Museum, Cirencester. How, I wonder, would William Deedes (the editor of that organ of middle-class respectability) justify such lavish coverage? An event of natural importance? An occasion of genuine sociological interest? Hardly, for the social sciences are rarely rated worth space in the Hartwell empire. Could it possibly be that people like Canon Arnold Nicholas of Wisbech and S.A.C. Francis of Chenderit School (contributors, on quite different matters, to the *Telegraph* letters page on the day of the funeral's exaltation) actually take a prurient interest in such events?

The Times thought the story worth only three eight-inch columns on page two. They appeared under the nostalgic headline 'Kray Funeral Recalls Old Days', and raised interesting questions of journalistic etiquette. In the body of Stewart Tendler's story, the Krays were subject to a strange social distinction. The Charles Krays (both junior and senior) were awarded the usual *Times* prefix of 'Mr'. But neither Ronald nor Reginald were afforded the usual courtesy. No doubt that was because 'handcuffed to prison officers, the two men, aged forty-eight, arrived in separate police vehicles.

The *Guardian* put the story on the front page under one of those cute headlines that clearly give pleasure to the sub-editors — 'Kray Funeral and the Gang's All There'. Frank Martin rivalled Kent Gavin and Peter Case of the *Mirror* for the day's best handcuff photograph. In the middle of Nick Davies's account of the day's events, we were promised 'more pictures on page two'. All human (or very nearly) life was there. Diana Dors — who, photographed from the front, appeared to be wearing a black mourning singlet rivalled Charles Kray senior, who was pictured holding up his trousers with both hands as if the police had removed his belt and braces.

It was Mr Davies who revealed why serious and respectable papers gave so much space to the most recent Kray incarceration. 'The Kray twins,' the story began, 'said farewell to their mother yesterday with a short poem, two hymns, more than three hundred wreaths, a thousand spectators and a lot of men in dark suits.' Compare Paul Callan in the *Mirror* 'The organ was moaning *The Lord Is My Shepherd* when Ronnie and Reggie were gently tugged by the handcuff ...') or Stewart Tendler of *The Times*. Mr Tendler — like his competitors on other papers — clearly thought that he had found the opportunity for a little fine writing. 'There were large muscular men with watchful eyes and faces no one could quite place,' he told us.

The desire to record memorable occasions memorably is an honourable journalistic ambition. So is the desire to capture interest for an inconsequential incident with the quality of the writing by which it is described. But elevating the Krays to the status of a national institution can be justified against neither criterion. Hence the built-in apology that appeared in every story and the right of the *Sun* to have the last word: ' . . .pure Cockney theatre and the reek of hypocrisy'.

Hard Pressed

WHAT WOULD HAPPEN if Fiona Richmond's scenery fell down? That is a question which has long obsessed me and I was, therefore, fascinated to read an account of such a disaster in the 26th Annual Report of the Press Council — a document which came through my letter-box last week. As Chapter 3,

'Outline of Council Adjudications', deals in some detail with the case of Cannock Chase District Councillors versus Keith Waterhouse of the *Daily Mirror*, prudence requires me to explain that it is four years since the *Sun* described the collapse of Miss Richmond's flies and flats.

For Mr Waterhouse was censured for implying that the behaviour of the Cannock council was 'pettifogging and nit-picking' in October 1978, when he could only justify the contention that they had been pettifogging and nit-picking in September 1976. The Press Council is not so anxious about keeping up to date. The 'current' annual report covers the Council's work in 1979.

It was during that year that John Hill of the *Sun* reported (at least according to the Press Council) that 'on the opening night at Harlow, scenery collapsed, lines were forgotten, costume changes went awry and a young couple walked out shouting Rubbish . . . Miss Richmond claimed that she had been misquoted and the inaccuracies which had been drawn to the *Sun's* attention were not corrected.

Regular readers of this column will easily imagine the relief with which I discovered that the *Sun* was exonerated. The notes of the news agency reporter who covered the show were examined. The head of his agency (who happened also to be at the first night, thought no doubt as a private citizen with a ticket for which he had himself paid) confirmed that when the show's director told customers, who believed themselves to be at a real performance, that they were watching a dress rehearsal and 'offered refunds, many went to the box office'. On the assumption that they made the journey for reasons other than an uncontrollable desire to congratulate the management and staff, the *Sun* seems to have had no case to answer.

But — as BBC investigative reporters always say when they cannot quite nail the miscreant, even though they decided that he was guilty before the sleuthing began — one worrying fact remains. Henry Douglas, the *Sun's* legal manager, 'said it seemed the *Sun* was in error in saying that scenery collapsed otherwise its report was amply documented.' The mystery of the missing full stop (which before its theft made the previous sentence almost literate and comprehensible) may never be solved. But, the Press Council's adjudication on the Richmond case does give us some sort of clue about what standards of accuracy they expect from newspapers.

The complaint against the *Sun* was rejected. 'The newspaper was entitled to criticize the production and the Press Council is not satisfied that there were any substantial inaccuracies in the report' — apart, they might have added, from saying that the scenery fell down when, as the *Sun's* own lawyer eventually agreed, it remained (consistent with the best traditions of Miss Richmond's performances) erect all night.

I know nothing of the standards of the stage. But it does seem to me that the collapse of scenery during a production is an enormity at once so spectacular and specific that its occurrence must alter a critic's whole judgement of the show. More important — assuming the play in question neither contained an earthquake scene nor was set in the London Blitz — I cannot imagine how Mr Hill, or the agency reporter who contributed to his column, believed that the scenery collapsed when it did no such thing. Yet the Press Council *seemed* to be saying that as it was generally agreed that the Fiona Richmond show was a catastrophe, the details of the chaos hardly mattered.

I do not wish to suggest that the Press Council is the type of permissive judge about whom the *Daily Express* would complain or the sort of pinko liberal that the *Daily Mail* would never allow to hawk a compassionate conscience in the jury box. The *Daily Express* is judged to have published a 'misleading and harmful' allegation 'that a mother and children had jumped a housing queue'. Its failure to correct the error 'was condemned'.

The *Daily Mail* was censured for a 'glaring example of improper journalism by innuendo' when it wrongly implied that a television personality was emotionally entangled with a Granada producer. Neither paper visibly reeled under the blow of either censure or condemnation.

In fact the Press Council, in that it has any power at all, acts as an emollient — convincing aggrieved persons that a sort of justice has been done and providing a just plausible alternative to some system of real surveillance and proper punishment. The Press Council protects the Press not the public. And there will be those who argue that in a free society that function in itself justifies the existence of a body which may be the last bastion between independent journalism and the onrush of totalitarian control.

In the year with which the 'current' Press Council dealt, there was a flurry of political concern about newspaper behaviour, the *Daily Telegraph* was excoriated for buying a witness's story before he gave incriminating evidence. James Kirkup was convicted of publishing a 'blasphemous' poem in *Gay News*. The European Court of Human Rights supported the *Sunday Times* decision to tell the Thalidomide story.

Three journalists (known as 'ABC') had official Secrets Act convictions (for reporting on 'Colonel B') quashed. As a result of the Council's Chairman speculates in his foreward about 'pains and penalties' as an alternative to 'persuasion'. Of course, he chooses the second alternative. But the British Press also needs constant scrutiny. That, Press Gang (in its modest way) will attempt to provide in 1983.

Within
the
Fringe

Spark Plugs

LAST TUESDAY, WHILST travelling uncomfortably by tube, I was delighted to observe that the man sitting opposite to me was holding before him a current copy of *Punch*. Suave, civilized and sophisticated, he looked the epitome of all the virtues which I associate with the magazine's regular readers. So pride jostled with pleasure as I noticed him literally licking his lips with apparent satisfaction as he concentrated on the contents of what I hoped was page eight-hundred-and-thirty-six.

When I left the train at Westminster Station, I peered through the carriage window to confirm that it was 'Press Gang' which held him in thrall. Over his pin-striped shoulder, I saw colour pictures of two girls — both in positions of naked abandon which at first led me to believe that the photographs had been taken for some sort of medical textbook. Then, when I noticed the name *Fiesta*, I could escape the awful truth no longer. The gentleman was hiding a 'girlie magazine' behind George Melly, William F. Buckley Jnr, Hunter Davies, Richard Gordon and me.

Before you could say 'Mind the doors' I realized that any magazine that relegated our combined talents to the status of camouflage must possess some special virtue. So, putting aside all concern about the damage that might be done to *Punch's* circulation, I determined to write, this week, about flesh, and made my immediate way to a nearby newsagent.

In Birmingham, the subterranean kiosk to which I sometimes make my furtive way puts its dirty books into brown paper-bags before it passes them across the counter. Indeed, I have often wished that they offered refuge in a similar subterfuge to chocolate addicts who have to smuggle their contraband past the diet police. But I noticed from the treatment meted out to a previous clean-raincoated purchaser, that in Horseferry Road, the newsagents believe in the courage of their customers' convictions.

I had just braced myself to make the brazen request when a couple of young Conservative backbenchers made their jolly way into the shop. Conscious of the courageous integrity required of a ruthless seeker after Press truth, I chose my magazine, paid my seventy pence and strode, head high, from the shop to write about my purchase.

Everyday Electronics is 'published approximately the third Friday of each month by IPC Magazines Ltd'. It contains a number of articles which, at first glance, might be assumed to hold the interest of my travelling companion to the point at which he journeyed on, engrossed, beyond his proper destination. But on a closer inspection both 'Heads and Tails Game' and 'Photo Flash Slave' turned out to be 'simple projects . . . selected to provide a wide range of subject and field of interest'. To my relief, the 'Popular Design' supplement ended with a note to 'newcomers to electronics' referring them to page 682 for 'general information'.

According to Fred Bennett, the editor of *Everyday Electronics*, his magazine sells 70,000 copies of each issue — rather more than the combined circulation of the *New Statesman*, *Spectator*, and *Listener*. And every station bookstall is crammed with equally esoteric publications. Indeed, as compared with the recherché range of periodicals that is to be found in some Smiths and many Menzies, *Everyday Electronics* deals with a positively homely subject. After all, as Mr Bennett himself says, we live in the electronics age. What more natural than that 'enthusiasts from ten through to four score' should want to build their own damp locator or opto alarm — 'a single-transistor circuit . . . designed to sound a minature audible warning device.'

In fact 'whether you intend to make a career out of it or indulge in it for amusement, or maybe profit, in your leisure, electronics is a very worthwhile subject to study.' Obviously, no one buys *Everyday Electronics* for the quality of its English. But it commands — particularly amongst the 'home construction enthusiasts' — the sort of specialised readership upon which IPC's profits are built. It is carefully constructed both to maintain the readership and to maximize the profit — not least by offering advertisers page after page of copy that amounts to direct plugs for their products.

'Teach-in 82' by O.N.Bishop (basic electronic theory with experiments') lists the 'components required for experiments' and actually announces that they 'may be obtained from the retailers listed on page 670'. That page turns out to be called 'Shop Talk', a column that manages to urge the purchase of items that range from the '*Verobloc* solderless breadbanding system module' to storage bins from *Link Hampson*'. Even the editorial manages to mention the twentieth anniversary of Vero Precision Engineering Limited and rejoices that 'today's thriving pastime of electronics has been built literally on Veroboard'. There are also thirty-one pages of orthodox advertising within the seventy-three pages of the magazine.

However, that — and the diagrams — aside *Everyday Electronics* contains one compelling ingredient — its subject. In the hope of making some sort of sense out of such assertions as 'a thyristor is a unilateral device and it will therefore only function properly if fed with a voltage of the correct polarity', I made my methodical way through O.N.Bishop's 'Basic Electronic Theory with Experiments', rejoicing in the *Boy's Own Paper* quality of both the initialled author and the use of the word 'experiment' to describe an exercise of which the outcome is not, to the slightest degree, in doubt. As I moved from 'Electic Charge' to 'Combining Resistances', I was horrified by the way the article sustained my interest.

My formal education ended long before C.P.Snow attempted to reconcile the two cultures, and I tried to justify parts of my misspent youth with jokes about the aesthetic inadequacy of mechanical scientists who spent their days in laboratories rather talking and drinking. In those days I felt intellectually superior to Isaac Newton since his business was numbers not words. Indeed, I still feel a sneaking guilt at being seduced by both 'good and bad conductors'. In fact, if you ever see me on the tube apparently reading *Fiesta*, there will probably be a copy of *Everyday Electronics* concealed inside.

Sinking Star

YOU MAY RECALL that some weeks ago a Russian submarine found itself embarrassingly un-submerged on a mud bank well inside Swedish territorial waters. Naturally enough, the incident occupied much space in British newspapers:

'One of the puzzling things about the Soviet submarine

stranded on the mud . . . only 10 miles from the main Swedish naval base of Karlskrona is that it is an absurdly obsolete vessel . . . It is said to be so unsuitable for spying that experts of the Royal Navy have compared the noise it makes under water to "a tube train in a tunnel" . . . The history of sea navigation since ancient times knows quite a number of such cases.'

That double defence of Soviet Submarine 137 is an apologia cobbled together by the admittedly malicious amalgamation of an item which appeared in the Peter Simple column of the *Daily Telegraph* on November 3rd and a news story published in the *Morning Star* nine days later. Assiduous students of the two papers will be able to see the join. The uninitiated will deduce where satire ends and double talk takes over by marking the spot where the English language degenerates into the sounds made by *Pravda* and talking weighing machines.

The *Morning Star* is the most illiterate and least successful newspaper in Britain. Indeed, in reality it is so illiterate and so unsuccessful that it is not a newspaper at all but a propaganda sheet which survives because it exists independently of the disciplines that govern normal national dailies. Principal amongst theose obligations is the necessity to put together a product sufficiently attractive to keep itself in commercial business. If the *Morning Star* had to break near to even, its readers would be denied the full text of the message sent by the Central Committee of the Soviet Communist Party to the 37th Congress of their British counterparts and the transcript of Leonid Brezhnev's interview with *Der Spiegel* magazine.

Of course, thanks to the dialectic devotion to Russia and the British Communist Party the *Morning Star* is able to rely on resources that a real newspaper could not top. Its 'Advertising Supplement' of November 6th can only be compared with the bill boards that cricket fanatics pay to erect round Test Match grounds. Drumming up business is the subsidiary objective. The real purpose is the provision of a hidden subsidy. So around Pyotor Abrarmov's article on the 1917 *Decree on Peace* and Vasily Stepanov's description of the eleventh five-year plan, *V-O Machinoexport, Baikal*

106

hunting guns and *Licensintorg* ('in practically every field of production and technology') plied their wares. We have no way of knowing how much business the expenditure promoted.

The second subsidy that the *Morning Star* enjoy is, of course, the donations of the faithful. The paper survives — though it does not thrive — on a depressingly circular process. The crude political bias and humourless obsession with the ideological view of literature and life repels the intellectually fastidious. But it is also used as a justification for demanding the unswerving support of the politically committed. 'The Rothermere-Murdoch-Matthews mafia know how to use their press power in aid of industrial tyrants like Edwardes and political tyrants like Thatcher . . . So let's pull out all the stops to get the *Star* message across on common cause with the just demands of BL workers.'

One of the stops on the *Morning Star's* keyboard is labelled 'money'. Each year the paper works out the tithes and tributes it must collect from its faithful flock to fill the gap between expenses and income. Rarely, if ever, is the target met. But a running total of comradely generosity is published each week together with entreaties to help make up the difference between socialist solvency and capitalist collapse. A collection of £2,200 at this year's TUC and another of £1,770 at the Scottish Trade Union Congress helped to ward off what the *bourgeoise* call bankruptcy.

Promoting the paper as if it was a weapon in the class war does little for circulation. That fell (according to the *Morning Star's* own figures) from an average daily sale of 33,792 during the first six months of 1980 to 32,770 in the first half of 1981. And the total would not have even been held at that figure without the mysterious 'foreign sales' that provide a third artificial source of income.

Of course, political purity denies to the *Morning Star* the sort of sales promotion techniques that are launched in the presence of 'all the media vultures, . . . there for the pickings at a boozy Fleet Street do.' Not for the disciples of socialist realism a colour magazine or a bingo competition. Even if such manifestations of Western decadence were acceptable, it is difficult to imagine the solemn stakhanavites making a success of either venture. The supplement would entire new readers with pictures of pig production on collective farms. And searching to match the *Daily Mail's* determination to call 'housy-housy' by a more acceptable name, they might well feel that the 'foreign sales' and bogus advertising would both be helped if they named their game of change 'Russian roulette'.

But the charge against the *Morning Star* is more than the accusation that it is grey and graceless. The indictment is that it is dishonest as well as dull, corrupt as well as crude. It uses the English language not to inform or delight but as a vehicle for unremitting propaganda, pretending that *Isvestia* communiqués are real news and that the *Tass* account of life in the Soviet Union approximates to the objective truth. The *Morning Star* has one redeeming feature. Since it is even more boring than it is biased it is more of a joke than a threat.

That single virtue can hardly be recorded in the Golden Book on the credit side of the Editor's account. And the debit column is very long indeed. Consider October 26th and accept (whatever your views on unilateral nuclear disarmament) that the peace demonstrations that took place the previous day commanded the support of millions of honestly-intentioned men and women anxious to end the arms race. The *Morning Star* reported that

> 'Near Berlin over 50,000 people attended a peace rally . . . calling for recognition of the constructive initiatives of the Soviet Union and other Socialist countries to strengthen peace and security.'

I am sure that story is true and that the Potsdam demonstrators actually believed all the slogans on their banners. But that was because they only read newspapers that operate on the same principles as the *Morning Star* — papers which exploit genuinely-held convictions, parody deeply-felt beliefs and, since they only exist as instruments of indoctrination, are not really newspapers at all.

Vox Pulp

TO THE SUPERFICIAL observer it may seem that *Militant, Fiesta* and *Titbits* have too little in common to make serious comparison possible. They never lie, even uneasily, beside each other on bookstalls. For *Militant* is sold on street corners by short-haired youths in sleeveless pullovers and training shoes whilst *Fiesta* is passed across sleazy newsagents' counters in incriminatingly anonymous brown-paper bags, and *Titbits* grins vacuously from the front of every W.H. Smith bookstand. *Fiesta* is full of crudely explicit accounts of sexual exploits, whilst *Militant* is crammed with eye-witness reports of the way in which Trotskyites protected the interests of working people and their families. *Titbits* specialises in features like 'Diana Ross — I may go blind'. Yet the three magazines have a common literary distinction. I have attempted to write a Press Gang column about all of them. And in each case I have found that both style and content defeated my attempts at serious comment.

I admit that I approached *Fiesta* in a mood which was not wholly conducive to contemplative writing. For the conventionally respectable student of the British press, acquiring a copy of the magazine is a traumatic experience. I made several dummy runs in the direction of a Birmingham subway bookstall before I worked out the easy way of making the purchase. Peter Riddell, the Political Editor of the *Financial Times*, was in town at the time of my research, covering the local election campaign. I persuaded him, together with Councillor Jim Ferguson (another figure of obvious probity), to accompany me to the counter and vouch, as necessary, for my academic intentions. Unfortunately both my minders deserted me within a few yards of the kiosk.

I was served by an elderly lady who looked as if she lived in a thatched cottage and divided her evenings between crocheting counterpanes and looking after her grand-children. I cannot recall how much I paid. But having pressed a number of coins into her hand, I stumbled to what I began to think of as my seedy hotel room. The lonely experience which followed was deeply degrading — to any member of the NUJ. All *Fiesta* sentences were the same. And all of its pictures portrayed the same parts of the human anatomy. As this is for family reading I will neither quote a single sentence, nor describe a solitary picture.

Buying *Militant* was not a problem. On average, I speak at three political meetings each week, and the path to half of them is picketed by earnest young men and women. They urge me to spend twenty pence from what they clearly believe to be my inherited fortune on 'The Marxist Paper for Labour and Youth'. I occasionally oblige. But when I read the rewards of my reckless expenditure, I always suspect that I have been sold last month's (or last year's) issue. On July 21 we were reminded of 'When the Right Wing Hounded Bevan'. A week later there was a warning about 'The Witch Hunt and Labour's Left', followed on July 16 with the doleful news that 'The Witch Hunt Spreads'.

Accounts of *Militant's* persecution are augmented by denunciation of the traitors within Labour's midst, and accounts of the international struggle against the forces of reaction. 'The Government of India under Indira Gandhi in its bid to protect capitalists' interests . . . ' is matched by 'The Right Wing and their Friends'. *Militant* supports strikes as a way of life and insists that 'The TUC must call a one-day General Strike'.

Occasionally, the pages of unremitting propaganda are relieved by a concession to 'culture'. In the issue of July 16th, Film Review assessed the merits of *Rosie the Riveter*. The opening paragraph deserves a wider audience than *Militant's* tiny circulation makes possible. 'All comrades should try to see this film. It provides an excellent basis for discussion on unemployment, both male and female.'

My political complaint against *Militant* is that it debases honourable causes. But on these pages I must be only interested in *Militant* the newspaper. Supporters of the 'tendency' which bears the same name insist that they are neither a party within a party nor the disciples of a distinct ideology. *Militant*, they say, is a fan magazine — but, uniquely, the readers are fans of the magazine itself. If that is how they wish their news-sheet to be judged, so be it. *Militant* is tedious, predictable, and wholly unconvincing. It is inconceivable that any normal person would buy it for pleasure. I can only assume that the continuous revolutionaries make their conversions first and distribute their paper afterwards. Anyone with a remotely open mind must find *Militant* either revolting or ridiculous.

Titbits is neither of those things. Indeed, it possesses no major characteristics at all. Its pin-ups point their charms at readers from the discreet protection of string vests, and it specializes in cartoons about demanding mothers-in-law and tactless children. And it gives its readers the inside stories of the stars. Barry Manilow, for instance, is 'considering putting his superstar career into second place — to become a dad'. And 'Richard Attenborough has . . . mortgaged his super house in Surrey to fulfil a mission in his life'. Believe it or not, Marilyn Monroe 'may well have had an affair with Einstein'. But the further the reader goes towards the back of the magazine, the naughtier ('naughty' is a *Titbits* word) it becomes. In the special summer edition, Edwin Kemp reviewed the careers of 'Masters of Sex' on page 63. By page 85, the advertisements were offering 'Mary Millington at her naughtiest on film and in these photo magazines'.

Presumably each of these three extraordinary publications meets some sort of need. Two of them actually make money and no doubt provide a measure of therapy or pleasure in the process. They are part of the eccentric way of the eclectic British Press and, in their different ways, proclaim both the virtues and the vices of a free society. Any one of them could be used as a text for a sermon concerning either the bliss of liberty or the degradation of materialism. But I think of each one in simpler terms. They are a waste of wood pulp. The idea of chopping down trees to produce such rubbish horrifies me.

Pride and Prejudice

I CAN NEVER remember how many words a single picture is supposed to be worth. I have blocked the equation out of my mind. For, it seems to me, whatever the truth of the arithmetical adage, it is necessary to suppress the notion that a single wink of the shutter may, in some cases, be superior to a thousand assiduously assembled adjectives, adverbs and nouns. However, there are moments when news of the world in the best, and therefore not the capitalized, usage of that phrase only comes to life when we actually see what is happening. And if the pictures are in colour and move, the armchair observer — although still under the influence of the people who edited his evening ration of *cinéma vérité* —actively feels the bomb-blast in his living room.

There are those who argue that it was the fear that reality would prove less popular than patriotic sentiment which caused the Ministry of Defence to delay the return of television film from the Falklands. Beirut (being both nearer to Britain and outside the jurisdiction of MoD information officers) has been bombed and shelled over supper for night after night. And the television reports on what has happened in that unhappy city have had a greater effect on me — and on my prejudices — than all the hundreds of column inches that have been written on the sad subject.

First it was the death, destruction and despair — havoc wrought amongst civilians who were irrelevant to the objectives and interests of the warring armies. Like me, they were witnesses to the conflict, not participants. But they were unlucky enough to occupy vantage points within range of the air-to-ground rockets and the mortar shells. Seeing the mutilated children in the half-demolished hospitals and the starving old women queueing for Red Cross water and United Nations milk-powder was an agonizing experience for those of us who love and admire Israel. When the PLO marched down to the docks on the first stage of their journey to assorted friendly countries, it was a positive relief to see how much of an army they had become. Those of us who thought — and still think — of the foundation of the Jewish national state as the great heroic act of the twentieth century needed a shred of justification, a mitigating circumstance no matter how small. The uniformed, disciplined, mechanized, automatic weapon-carrying legions almost provided it. Or, at least, appeared to do so on television.

If the whole Lebanese horror has bitten into the conscience and undermined the confidence of friendly Gentiles, how much greater the trauma must have been for rational and compassionate Jews — especially those whose duty it was to report on the behaviour of Menachem Begin's government in general and Defence Minister Ariel Sharon in particular.

On the evidence of the stories published in the *Jewish Chronicle,* at least some of them got within an honourable distance of objectivity; allowing, that is, for their undoubted feeling that Israel was at war with a force which exists only to destroy the homeland that has been the dream of the Jewish people for almost two thousand years.

Of course, the battle of objective reporting was not waged with uniform ferocity. Jenni Frazer, writing on August 13th under the headline 'Anger at MPs' Outbursts' began her story: 'Widespread condemnation has been expressed in the Jewish community this week following two controversial statements made by Jewish MPs about the Lebanon war'. The only criticism which was actually quoted was from 'the Board of Deputies and the Zionist Federation'. I am assured that in Hebrew — that most precise of languages — 'Jewish community' and 'Board of Deputies' are not synonymous. The point was underlined by the Board's criticism of the dissenting MPs who, it alleged, were Jewish by race but not by religious observance.

On July 23rd Joseph Finklestone's front-page lead began with a wholly acceptable paragraph. 'A Russian plan to land Soviet troops in Lebanon in the event of an emergency in which the United States became involved *could* be the explanation why such huge stocks of arms were assembled at PLO bases in Lebanon *according to Mr Gideon Platt, the Israeli Minister of Industry and Commerce.'* The italics are mine. Unfortunately, the sub-editors failed to notice the words which I emphasize. As a result, the headline read, 'Russia planned to send troops to Lebanon'. There were no quotation marks to explain that what followed was a report of allegations made during 'an interview . . . this week'. From a distance it looked like a *Jewish Chronicle* world scoop and a justification for massive and immediate military action.

But the correspondents contributing from Israel filed stories which were properly tinged with the iconoclasm that is essential to a free press. 'Menachem Begin . . . has so far succeeded in stifling controversy within the Cabinet,' wrote Yoram Kessel from Jerusalem. 'Officials here are carefully nurturing the impression that it was not, as Washington contends, American pressure which led to the ending of Israel's bombardment.' Politicians a great deal cooler than Mr Begin find words like 'stifling' and 'nurturing' infuriatingly offensive. They carry the implication of political manipulation. And there is always the suspicion that the implication was intentional.

Of course, intentions can easily be mistaken. 'BBC television,' the *Jewish Chronicle* told us on July 16th, 'provided film evidence and voice commentary to suggest why civilian apartment blocks in West Beirut could be considered legitimate targets.' I regard the choice of the conditional 'could' and the use of the verb 'to suggest' as signs of grace. But the message that the moving pictures sent to the *Jewish Chronicle* was not the same as the one which they sent to me. With only words to rely on, I too might have believed in the justice of Israel's cause. After the television reports, I can only echo the opinion expressed by one of the 'condemned' MPs. Presenting Israel's case is becoming increasingly difficult — see any recent edition of the *Jewish Chronicle*.

Rural Reads

IT WAS *HAMPSHIRE* which caught and held my attention. I have known for years that 'county magazines' are published every month. Indeed, they had smiled at me from railway station bookstalls ever since the days when *The Times* had classified advertisements on its front page and the *Magnet* chronicled the life and work of Billy Bunter. But although I have felt a moment's admiration for the pictures of glossy Arcadia which grace their covers, until this summer I was innocent of what lay beneath the full panorama of stately homes, noble piles and sunken gardens, open to the public for a week in aid of Doctor Barnado's Homes. Now I have read *Warwickshire and Worcestershire Life* ('including West Midlands'), *Lancashire Life* (including Furness, Greater Manchester and Merseyside') and *Cheshire Life* (including Wirral and South Manchester') from cover to cover. And I blame it all on

114

Hampshire ('incorporating Bournemouth and Christchurch').

I found the cover story of the July issue irresistible. Beneath a photograph of 'cottage by the stream at Selbourne' was the titillating announcement: 'Argentine dictator makes his home in Southampton'. Ignorant of that city's geography, I naively assumed Selbourne to be one of its suburbs and the cottage to have been the dictator's refuge. Lucky indeed the tin-pot tyrant who lived beneath the mossy roof and looked through the mullioned windows at the great unregimented beds of tousled flowers. Only an idiot would have exchanged the honey-suckle for two hundred per cent annual inflation and precarious membership of a military junta. It was worth fifty pence to discover the lunatic's name.

The dictator to which the 'come on' referred was General Juan Manuel de Rosas; and if you have never heard of him, do not blame your daily paper's coverage of the Falklands crisis. For he lived in Southampton between 1852 and 1861 in a Victorian villa which now houses the Social Security Appeals Tribunal. The cottage on the cover had nothing to do with the story which was advertised beneath it. I make no complaint about that. My mistaken belief that the picture was related to the prose lured me inside the magazine.

Now I always buy the 'county magazines' when I am marooned in rural parts. They are packed with historical anecdotes which delight my second-rate antiquarian mind and they abound with pictures of the market-crosses, tithe-barns and lych-gates that sentimental townies like me think of as the essence of England.

Take the General de Rosas story for example. I am naturally attracted to anyone who wins an election (no matter how crooked) by 9,315 to 5. And I felt an immediate sympathy for those of the supporters who erected 'a polished pink marble obelisk' in his honour. News of its renovation in 1972 filled me with a different emotion. The conservationists also 'secured the annulment of the 1861 resolution of the Argentine Congress' which condemned their hero 'as a mass murderer. It specified 2,034 assassinations ... although he may have been responsible for ten times as many.' Until I am certain that the General de Rosas Appreciation Society has left Southampton, I shall travel no further south than Winchester.

So I shall not visit the villages on the banks of the River Test which, if *Hampshire's* pictures are to be believed, 'still delight the eye', or see the windmill at Bursledon where Nelson's Copenhagen flagship was built. I shall turn instead to other local glories from our national history as revealed in the pages of the country magazines - the parish church at Areley Kings (a *Warwickshire and Worcestershire* village of the month), Hamilton Square in Birkenhead (as portrayed in *Cheshire Life*) or Lord Derby's seaside cottage turned into a (*Lancashire*) hotel. The county magazines are inconsequential guide-books for journeys of trivial exploration. Long may their pride in the local past continue.

It has, of course, to be kept within reasonable limits. 'Most people inevitably link the name of Sir Walter Scott — who died 150 years ago this month — with the novel *Kenilworth*', is essentially an extract from the Warwickshire school of literary criticism. But such excesses of local patriotism are not the greatest fault of all the county magazines. The truth is that the Whitethorn Press (which publishes *Lancashire, Cheshire, Warwickshire and Worcestershire, Gloucestershire and Avon* and *Yorkshire Life*) has elevated snobbery into an art form. The trick is performed by the juxtaposition of items concerning two distant social groups — the haves (Lady Cobham, 'the driving force behind the promotion of Hagley Hall' and the Duke of Westminster, 'reported to have bought a forty-five ton Churchill tank') and the wish-we-had-as-wells. The second group is photographed whilst being married or raising money for charity.

Thus we see Mr Chris Denniston (who has adopted the *Brideshead Revisited* style of evening dress) 'chatting to Mr Richard Myrtle' at the 'ball in aid of the British Heart Foundation' and 'Nicholas Owen, only son of Mr and Mrs R. O. Owen of Wallasey', wearing a similar celluloid collar on the occasion of his marriage to 'Heather Lloyd, youngest daughter of Mrs Stewart of Upton', who appears to have retaliated by turning up at the church in a bathing costume. Many pages are naturally devoted to the good life — eating out, fitted kitchens and sports cars. Horses and antiques add a note of old-world class.

But there are genuine memories of the real old England to counterbalance the meretricious articles about dealing with a troublesome hairdresser and the growing fashion of riding side-saddle. The story of the 1896 mass trespass that kept the Lancashire footpaths open is as much part of the country's history as any tale of the Earls of Derby. And Henry Mortimer has done more for Cheshire's reputation than most of the residents at Eaton Hall have managed. The truth of the matter is that England is so various a country that all its counties contain enough material for a thousand interesting articles. The county magazines manage to publish two or three each month. With even so low a ratio, I am grateful to *Hampshire* for the new pleasures it has revealed.

Sporting Type

FOR HALF A dozen post-war winters my Saturday evenings all began in the same way. At half-past six I invariably stood outside a cottage at the corner of Laird and Worrall roads. The cottage had been crudely converted into a paper shop and at seven o'clock on Saturday nights the newsagents of Sheffield received copies of the *Green 'Un*. I arrived anxious and early, afraid that if I was not at the front of the queue the local football special — printed, as its name implied, on paper the colour of weak pea soup — would be sold out.

The front page news — concerning the performance of Sheffield Wednesday — was already known to me. If the 'Owls' had been at home that afternoon, I would have watched every scintillating second of the pulsating ninety-minute game. And if they had played away I would have stood on Sheffield United's terraces, not concentrating on the 'Blades' and their opponents but waiting for the news of goals on distant grounds to be hung on the board. Wednesday supporters went to Bramhall Lane to see 'how Wednesday were getting on'. And, of course, I would have heard the results confirmed on the radio. But although I knew the score I wanted to read it again in the *Green 'Un*.

Even when I had actually watched the game from the windy heights of Spion Kop, I still wanted to read the accounts of what I had seen as written by the *Green 'Un's* part-time journalists. The view from the top of the terrace did not allow the spectator to absorb the nuances of play. Fred Walters (Fred 'Wednesday' Walters as his United supporting detractors called him) was able to fill in the details — how Joe Cockcroft had deflected the ball before it entered the Owls' net, and why Hugh Swift had missed his tackle against the opposing right wing.

The *Green 'Un* also described a game which, whilst based on the match I had seen, elevated the ninety minutes from play to poetry. Often it was very bad poetry. But when I read J. B. Priestley's description of Association Football as 'conflict and art' I assumed that he meant football as described by the *Green 'Un* on a Saturday night rather than as seen at the ground on a Saturday afternoon.

These days I rarely see Sheffield's *Green 'Un*. But I do (from time to time) visit other footballing towns and read their football specials. Last week it was Lancashire's turn to be lucky. In Manchester the *Evening News* publishes a 'New Super Pink Final'. Bolton prints its football paper on perfectly normal coloured paper. But such is the tradition of the coloured football extra that they call it the 'Sporting Buff'. If a pun is intended the second meaning is wholly appropriate, for it is written in a style — indeed a language — which only the enthusiast can understand. One of the irresistible features of the football special is that it speaks for, to and about the locality in which it is published. There are no concessions to the barbarians beyond the city boundaries. Those who do not speak the common language must accept the penalty of their ignorance.

Take, for instance, New Super Pink Final's comment on Oldham Athletic's management style — described by Pat Hince as faith, hope and charity. 'The faith', we were told, was displayed by 'the Lactics' first team coach'. Saint Paul being vindicated by an away draw, Mr Hince confirmed that the result was everything that 'the Boundary Park management team could have wished'. People (I agree, profoundly ignorant people) who neither know Oldam Athletic's nickname nor the address of the ground on which they play can hardly understand a word. The column is rightly written for the fans who look at 'Oldhams Check Chart' with a feeling of deep personal commitment.

Of course, the Lactics of Oldham appear on page fourteen. A Manchester paper must reserve its front page for the result tables and news of the two Mancunian giants. But again, the headline must have seemed, to the uninitiated, to be some sort of coded message — 'Battling Reds 0–0 — City held'. Of course, all decent people know that the 'Reds' are Manchester United and 'City' is Manchester City — the 'Blues'. But it is a closed community for which Steve McHugh caters. For all its record of slashed railway carriage seats and wrecked motorway cafes, it is a comforting camaraderie that the closed community provides. Not for nothing do they sing 'You'll Never Walk Alone'. Football specials are family papers. 'We will reap the reward,' writes Gordon Sharrock in his commentary on Bolton Wanderers' recent record of failure. His optimism is probably un-justified. But the collective personal pronoun is wholly appropriate.

Football extras are on the streets within a couple of hours of full time; so they pose particular production problems. Super Pink overcomes the difficulty by printing a twenty-four page 'magazine' of comment and analysis during the earlier part of the week and wrapping it in eight pages of Saturday's sporting news. Even so, it needs a special sort of journalistic ingenuity to produce the football stories in time. David Meek ('at Anfield') gives a brilliant exhibition of the art of reporting a football match whilst it is still being played. 'But,' his story concludes, 'full marks to United's defence, Bailey in particular, for keeping Liverpool at bay.'

I would gamble both my blue and white rosette and owl motif sweater that the apparent final judgement was written before full time — say, after sixty-five minutes whilst the score sheet was still blank.

On the front page Steve McHugh finished the story, secure in the knowledge that whether or not Bailey let one in, the Meek encomium would still apply. In fact, Bailey kept a clean sheet; vindicating the technique of both the professional goal keeper and the professional football writer, and making me feel again the provincial delights of supporting a northern football club.

In paradise I shall see Sheffield Wednesday play every

Saturday afternoon. When I graduate to heaven I shall get a free copy of the *Green 'Un* every Saturday night.

Book Ends

AT LEAST A thousand new books and re-issued classics are published in Britain during a normal literary week. Occasionally, two thousand titles are packed into a crowded seven days, each one with its own Standard Book Number and (if schoolboy mythology is to be believed) a place awaiting its arrival on the shelves of the British Museum. Each one is listed at the back of *The Bookseller* — 'the organ of the British book trade'. Some of them are not exactly candidates for the single volume that I would choose to take with me to a desert island (in addition to the Bible and the works of William Shakespeare) along with my eight records and my single luxury object.

No doubt the demand for *Agrarian Change and Household Organisation in the Loire Valley 1500–1900* is greater than at first assumed by those sceptics who first discovered its existence in *The Bookseller* of 25th September 1982. Otherwise Academic and University Publications would not have offered it to the reading public for £27.30. But I suspect that it will not sell as many copies as *Children Welcome!*, available at 95p from Herald Advisory Services and immortalized in *The Bookseller* on 5th February 1983.

Such information — together with the tables of Book Publishers' Output and the Academic and Professional Bulletin — are meant for the technical end of the trade. But buried in the other pages are items that gleam like gold in the dross of English letters and literature — revealing the nature of the British book-reading public and the character of British publishers in equally enthralling detail. Let us examine Weidenfeld & Nicolson, one of the more lavish advertisers, who spare no trouble to warn the bibliophiles of Britain about the host of recently-commissioned classics which are on their way into the bookshops.

Take January 27th, for instance. On that blessed day we

120

were promised 'the first work of world history to present truthfully, objectively and fully the whole period from the break-up of the old European system to the present day'. Its virtues were particularized in capital letters: VAST IN SCOPE — COMPREHENSIVE — FULLY DOCUMENTED — CONTROVERSIAL — HIGHLY READABLE — A WORK OF REFERENCE. After all that, it comes as something of a surprise to discover that it was written by Paul Johnson. The revelation provokes the more thoughtful of potential purchasers into further analysis.

A History of the Modern World covers the 63 years from 1917 to 1980. It 'deals with nearly 150 nations' and we will charitably assume that 'nearly 150' amounts to 149. It has 832 pages. According to my pocket calculator, that amounts to 5.5838926 pages per nation, or 0.0886332 pages per national year. Without my pocket calculator, I estimate that 0.08 of a page is about one-third of a line. That amounts, on average, to three-and-a-bit words per country per year — in which is incorporated 'the latest scholarship over a very wide field'.

The terrible revelation that appears on every page of *The Bookseller* is that publishers promote their product as if it were Pepsi-Cola and sell their output as if it were soap. And occasionally they talk about the commodities they sell as if they were new stock issues, to be judged according to their profit potential and to be described in the strange jargon of a sub-culture which is more numerate than literate. Consider Sarah Broadhurst on 'Paperback bestsellers for 1983'.

> 'The major mass-market leads are noted here, but of the big names — Maclean, Robbins, Archer and the like — I have said nothing; they speak for themselves ... Some, perhaps, are not obvious sellers nor known entities, but they will get full promotional treatment and perhaps become bestsellers. They are worth watching.'

Of course, there are some literary items. 'Booker 1982: surprises on the shortlist' promised something approaching criticism in a full-page article devoted to the six novels that made it to the last stage of the Booker-McConnell Prize selection. Its judgement was decisive:

> 'Hoping to repeat the raid on the shortlist of two years
> ago, when it managed to paperback and get into the
> bookshops before the winner was announced five of the
> seven short-listed titles, Penguin was quickly on the
> telephone to the publishers concerned

If you read that sentence two or three times for sense, you
will see that it aims to convey a message concerned with
marketing.

By now, the fair-minded amongst you will have begun to
complain that the weekly magazine which I describe is *The
Bookseller,* not *The Bookreader,* and that it is supposed to
provide 50 pence-worth of technical information for the
trade. I know. But I am entitled to write a little personal
threnody for the sort of publisher that employed T. S. Eliot
and the type of bookshop which rejoices in an owner who
enjoys being surrounded by books and is therefore only
vaguely interested in 'shelf-life' — indeed, is sorry to see the
books go and is, therefore, at best ambivalent about quick
turnover. Only the amateur psychologists amongst them
would be interested in the Book Marketing Council's report
on impulse buying (4th September 1982).

I nevertheless hasten to advise readers of books as well as
book salesmen to buy an occasional copy of *The Bookseller.*
In spirit it is, of course, more akin to *Farmers Weekly* than
The Times Literary Supplement and it makes no pretence of
being anything other than a trade paper. But its trade is
books and its pages are packed with little precis of the
contents of those precious commodities, coloured replicas of
jacket covers, portraits of authors and pictures of 'romances
so daring . . . stories so compelling . . . millions are waiting for
them.' It is a mighty catalogue of what should not be missed
— even by the people who write the copy for Weidenfeld &
Nicolson's advertisements.

Only
on
Sundays

Bloody Sunday

ACCORDING TO THE latest figures from the Audit Bureau of Circulation, 1981 has been a good year for the *Sunday Express*. Thanks largely to the introduction of a colour magazine, its average weekly sale has increased to 2,996,447 copies. To borrow a phrase from the triumphant newspaper, that figure represents 'two major achievements'. Forty thousand new recruits is, in itself, a justification for rejoicing. To have enlisted them at a time when other Sunday sales were in decline is exactly the sort of success that a newspaper likes to boast about on the front page.

Yet the *Sunday Express* chose to proclaim a different victory. Advertisers are attracted by the number of potential customers who cast their eyes across a paper's pages. And the bold black type announced the allegiance of 7,646,000 individual readers. But a price had to be paid for the promotion of that figure. 'The readership of the *Sunday Express,*' the small print said, 'remains stable' — a judgement of health and prosperity usually associated with intensive care units.

However, the comparison of the National Readership Surveys for 1980 and 1981 offered the *Sunday Express* the chance to claim two glittering prizes — an increase of 172,000 in its younger readers and 'yet more strength among the leaders of industry, commerce and the professions'. The conclusion "drawn from the figures" was obvious. *The Sunday Express* 'is ever increasingly becoming *the* newspaper of those at the top and the thrusting, intelligent young men and women on their way to the top.' We can only guess what it is about the paper that interests them — and the small rumber of stupid, lazy failures who also glance at it from time to time.

Undoubtedly, the *Sunday Express* creates a feeling of comfortable certainty. It does not spoil Sunday lunch by raising debilitating moral doubts or provoking indigestible intellectual dilemmas. In a changing and troubled world, it exudes the hopeful innocence of the early Fifties when Gay Gambol bought the little cocktail dresses that feature in the back page cartoon, and George still believed that Anthony Eden was the enemy of appeasement who would fight his way

125

to the far end of the Suez Canal.

Indeed, George Gambol is the *Sunday Express* man, with a (comparatively) innocent eye for the ladies, an obsession with portable property and a clear view of his place in respectable society. The only tragedies to have touched his life are the visits of unwelcome relatives and enforced gardening. He buys the *Sunday Express* for the lively sports coverage and rarely reads the front page lead. When he does notice 'Mrs T: My Fears for the Queen's Safety' or 'Guns All The Way On The Big Day' he never realizes that the story hardly ever justifies the banner headlines.

Nor will he find it very easy to describe the difference between what fell through his letter-box in, say, July 1979 and July of the *annus mirabilis*. Working his way through the paper he will find little on page two that revals the vintage of Lady Olga Maitland's Diary. Anyone who remembers when Jonathan Aitken lost his bachelor status or recalls the year of the Christina Onassis wedding might be able to calculate the date. But the rest of humanity must find the account of the Earl of Plymouth's 'amusing exchange with a lorry driver' as timeless as it is pointless.

Over the years, Scarth Flett and Peter Dacre have provided what is clearly intended to be a tantalizing glimpse of life amongst the stars. 'The man Virginia met as she was about to marry somebody else' and 'I didn't do the seducing in the back of that taxi' are variations on the same theme pitched at a level of titillation that might offend Grandma Giles but would not be unacceptable to country vets and small boat owners — two groups of persons who appear prominently on news and feature pages.

Indeed, the way that the *Sunday Express* treats sex has much in common with the supposed Victorian habit of covering piano legs with modest curtains. The veiled references to promiscuity and perversion owe more to prurience than puritanism. A perfect example appears in the John Junor column for July 1979 which announced that 'young Zulu maidens are subject to compulsory virginity tests' and ended with the usually arch assurances about the virility of men from Auchtermuchty. In addition to surreptitious sex, Sir John has a neat line in socially acceptable violence. 'Wouldn't it be marvellous,' he asked us to agree, 'if every time an IRA terrorist, strolling along a Dublin street, felt a tap on his shoulder, it turned out to be a British agent come to exact revenge?'

There can be little doubt that Sir John's character is clearly imprinted on the paper's every page. That can be the only possible explanation of both the obsession with sailing ('It's not just a rich man's sport. You too could own and crew an ocean racer') and the sentimental stories about animals that make their maudlin way into every issue. 'Lonely grouse stops woman motorist 200 times just to say hello' in July 1979 became 'All night vigil in a downpour saved Hoppy the limping badger' two years later.

At least, in animal stories, the species change from time to time. The girls in the news page photographs are all indistinguishable. Ruth Gleason 'splashing about in the sea', Faith Dakin 'a qualified parachutist', Beulah Hughes 'fighting the flab with water ski-ing' and Judi Gardiner 'with her neighbour's Pyrenean mountain dog' are all synthetically interchangeable. It seems unlikely that they are the reasons for the undying enthusiasm of 'thrusting, intelligent young men and women'. The hard truth is that the appeal has three main ingredients — first-class reporting of football and cricket, an all-pervading political prejudice and thousands of words that can pass effortlessly through the readers' minds without intruding too loudly on the television, the weekend gin-and-tonic, or the dreams of making it to the top.

Vox Pop

LAST FRIDAY, THE *Sunday People* celebrated its centenary with a dinner at the Dorchester Hotel. The invitation, suitably surmounted by both the 1881 and 1981 mast-heads, described the occasion as marking 'One hundred years of continuous publication'. That is a slight exaggeration. For, as I confirmed with the man who was Father of the NUJ Chapel at the time, faithful readers have spent desolate weekends denied their favourite paper 'as a result of industrial action'. But only the most carping critic would have remembered such depressing details in the Dorchester Ballroom last Friday night. We all rejoiced at the survival and success of an endearing as well as an enduring Fleet Street phenomenon — 'the newspaper for all classes'; triumphantly homely and unrepentantly confortable.

That does not mean that every edition consists entirely of 'Dreamalong with Max's Memories'. Indeed the last newspaper of the first century contained the most horrifically graphic account of the Chelsea bombing to be published on the sad Sunday morning that followed the IRA outrage. 'I picked up a uniform sleeve and saw there was an arm in it,' said the first off-duty Guardsman on the scene. And being a family paper the *Sunday People* reported that the victim's wife was 'expecting a baby any day now'.

Somehow the *Sunday People* managed to juxtapose the sensational story and the sentimental overtones without seeming mawkish. That is because the paper either really does care, or manages to give a brilliantly convincing imitation of continual compassion. Having had to contend with the editor's determination to protect his staff from what he feared might be the cheap jibes of the pseudo-sophisticated, I am inclined to believe it is all genuine. Perhaps I was brainwashed by the poster that claimed it to be 'The Family Paper that Fights For You'. But I believe it is, and I believe that it does.

Whether it has always done so is quite a different matter. Certainly the first issue — leading, like number 5203 a hundred years later, on Irish terrorism — had on its front page a sad tale of poverty, concerning an unemployed council workman who slit his throat rather than live on parish relief. But a quarter of a century ago, the paper had begun to swing in anticipation of the meretricious decade which was to follow. The headlines from October 1956 would not have been out of place this month — 'Poland in Revolt', 'Shirley Struggles Through Tears to Stardom' and 'Tony Will Shock Them'. But that year the city in turmoil was Warsaw not Gdansk. It was Shirley Bassey not Williams who wept her way to fame, and Tony Moynihan not Benn whose confession scandalized society.

And in those days the paper was harder as well as cruder. 'Today,' Gilbert Harding began his column on October 7th

1950, 'I would like to call for an urgent inquiry into the working of the meals service in our schools.' Perhaps (in choice of subject, if not in style) Mr Harding was years ahead of his time. But the rest of the paper, from the hat competition (featuring six photographs of the young Princess Margaret) to the expose of the 'Cripple Queues for His Cure' scandal, is more than dated. It has an obvious commercialism that today's paper manages to avoid.

Of course, at that time, the *People* was going through its 'Frank, Fearless and Free' stage — 'a searchlight ... manned by a team of crusading investigators whose ranks are constantly renewed.' No doubt public service was performed by the details Duncan Webb revealed of the Messina Brothers activities. Perhaps the same can be said for the exposure of the 'soccer bribes scandal' — though on the terraces at Hillsborough, there was not universal praise for the paper that sent three Sheffield Wednesday players to prison. But today the strident note has gone. Believe it or not, they even employ a calm, composed and slightly nervous Woman's Editor.

Patricia Boxall is, in my experience, unique amongst lady journalists in that she looks as young as the photograph at the top of her column. That is, of course, sexist observation for which she would gently chide me. But despite her absurd description as 'the woman columnist men can't ignore' she has aspirations to be neither Glenda Slag nor Joan of Arc. She cannot understand the compulsion to be 'bitchy' that clearly motivates some members of her trade, never attends fashionable occasions or glittering parties, and barely knows other Woman's Editors on other papers. She once met Lynda Lee-Potter on a bus when they were both travelling to Waterloo and she *thinks* that she attended a Woman of the Year Lunch at which Jean Rook was also present. But since the Dowager Doyen of Fleet Street was at the top table and Miss Boxall was in an annexe off the main room, their paths never crossed.

But, be not deceived. Despite the reticence and the rectitude, Miss Boxall is, in many ways, a more formidable figure than her overtly aggressive colleagues. Her strength lies in her enthusiasm to write for, and about, real women — not girls with orange hair and *Adam and the Ants* records, or

129

middle-aged matrons who want to grow up to become Joan Collins. Her readers take their washing to the launderette, worry about the cost of school meals and argue with their husbands about which paper best represents the interests of working women. If they read *Vogue* in the hairdressers they think of it as an uneasy compromise between a joke and a phantasy. They may find out what is in the Paris Spring Collection. But they have neither the financial ability nor the emotional enthusiasm to buy expensive copies.

In a very real sense Patricia Boxall typifies the spirit of the new paper that was born when it turned tabloid in 1974. It has abandoned the salacious interests and the deferential reverence of its broadsheet days. It is now about the decent practicalities of life; though they sometimes have to be dressed up to brighten Sunday morning. Like the readers for whom it hopes to cater, it is anxious to be 'nice'. Perhaps 'niceness' is not a major virtue. But it is not a bad principle on which to build a highly successful paper. Many Happy Returns.

Telegraph Lines

ON SUNDAY MORNINGS my wants are simple. All I need is tea, toast, the newspapers and freedom from exhortation to get washed. At home, my wish is usually granted. So I begin the day of rest with dressing-gown across knees, cup in hand, butter on face and colour supplements spread on the floor at my feet. Of course, I do not actually read the papers before lunch. The hard concentration comes after the stubble and the pyjamas have been removed and I have prepared myself for the intellectual rigours of Woodrow Wyatt's *Sunday Mirror* column by loosening up my mental muscles on *Principia Mathematica* and *Language, Truth and Logic*. In the morning, I just turn over the pages to make sure that, in Fleet Street, nothing has changed.

By the time the tea turns into coffee and the toast becomes a chocolate biscuit, I am content that the world is as it always was. Michael Watts is still padding out his column with items sent to him by *Sunday Express* readers. In the *Observer* Clive James continues his expedition to the outer limits of self-indulgence. Rustling my way through the whole spectrum of political correspondents from the sacred: (Hugo Young in the *Sunday Times*) to the profane (Gordon Leake in the *News of the World*) I sometimes forget that other readers are more selective. In discriminating households all over Britain, families are surviving on a single paper. Some of them actually choose the *Sunday Telegraph*.

Its attraction is easily described. From the assiduous and the methodical, it provides forty pages of tightly packed information. All of its opinions are offered, not in the authentic voice of the English Establishment but in the accents of a much larger potential readership — the men and women who yearn to possess a box at Ascot, long for a son at Eton and pine for a daughter who danced with the Prince of Wales. For them the 'Albany Column' with its penchant for Diplomatic Corps gossip is a vicarious glimpse inside the chancelleries of Europe. To them, the editorials grumble away in the language of disgruntled dowagers who have known better days. On their behalf the *Sunday Telegraph* employs a peer of the realm to write about the sport of kings and political pundits to meet every reactionary taste. The romantic right can identify with Peregrine Worsthorne, the cavalier of Conservative columnists. The duller diehards can fight their way through Graham Turner's turgid tales of industrial decline.

I have no wish to present a false picture of the men in 'genuine military sweaters (made to official specification)' and the women with single rows of cultured pearls ('direct from importers . . . with a written guarantee'). So I rely for my portrait on the people who ought to know, the contributors to its classified advertisement columns. Presumably, the merchants and manufacturers know where to find their natural market. *Sunday Telegraph* readers are the sort of people who buy the sort of things that the *Sunday Telegraph* helps to sell. 'Why knock holes in your door and waste energy?' asks Viking Products Ltd, presumably in the knowledge that the devotees of Wilf Wooller and Tony Lewis would find the temptation irresistible were it not for the availability of 'Danish style letterboxes'.

131

But the inclination to hack away at family woodwork must be one of the few reckless instincts harboured by *Sunday Telegraph* readers. Normally they are the most cautious of people who 'avoid nasty incidents' with Grippex which 'makes your shoes or boots slip proof', or Non-Slip snow spikes 'that make walking in snow and icy conditions easy and safe'. They protect themselves from burglaries with automatic 'off at dawn: on all night' lamps which 'provide security at a minimum cost' and avoid road accidents by the assiduous use of At-a-glance 'tyre pressure monitors'. With a personal torch alarm ('protect yourself and your valuables anytime, anywhere') in one pocket and a Be Warm personal heater ('face the coldest weather with confidence') in the other, the baggy tweeds may bulge, but the wearer will be ready for any *News of the World*-reading yobbos.

Of course, some *Sunday Telegraph* readers are less able to fight for their lives than when they went to WOSB. Beneath the 'storm shield coats (to clear, only £17.50)' and 'Men's Trousers For All', there is sometimes more than an 'undetectable wallet-belt — the safe way to carry your cash'. *Herniaflex* 'support slips on like trunks' and 'protective underwear in white and black latex' is available post free. Indeed, some of them have gone positively soft and possess deflatable bath-pillows which enable them to 'experience deep relaxation' while they 'soak in the bath' (£3.85 plus 30p p. and p.). Others have forgotten the 'no-nonsense' attitude towards health and hygiene which they were taught at prep school, and wear *Rumaton* magnetic bracelets and necklaces which make no claim to cure rheumatism but give sufferers a knowing nudge on their arthritic elbows as they boast superiority over 'copper and magnetic' ju-jus — in other words 'The original *Synoval Rumatica*, worn by top people and praised on radio'. Some of them have hair transplants at £275 per tonsure

Despite these physical vicissitudes, the *Sunday Telegraph* readers remain indomitably neat. They buy coffin-shaped polystyrene containers that enable them to store clothes under their beds, collapsible plastic wardrobes and 'handy boxes' that 'keep tools tidy' for £8.95. And, of course, their patriotism is beyond question or doubt. The Calendar of Historic London hangs on their walls and they keep their place in *Wisden's* with Royal Wedding Sterling Silver Book-marks. Occasionally, they go a little further than good taste allows and buy each other jokey gifts like bedspreads printed to look like Union Jacks and 'wooden loo seats . . . with your personal crest or monogram'. But usually they stick to sens-ible bargains and provident bulk buys. Above all, the *Sunday Telegraph* small ads are for careful people concerned with the protection of their own interests. The editorials are clearly designed to meet the same emotional need.

All Human Life

IF GRANADA TELEVISION makes a *What the Papers Say* award for the nastiest front page of the year, the *News of the World* will win a prize at last and Barry Askew, its new editor, will have another trophy to put on his mantelpiece alongside those that he acquired during his days of provincial innocence in Preston. On November 22nd his 'world scoop' was heralded by a headline which no other entrant in the 'nasty category' would be able to compete — 'My Dr Crippen Lover Tried to Poison Me Too'. And, as if to confirm the paper's unassailable superiority in any 'salacious section' that Granada might include within their competition, the salivating reader was then led into the story with the revela-tion that 'he slipped me the drug and then we made love'.

The following week the paper made a sudden literary lurch and had an allegory flapping immediately below its mast-head as the 'come on' for the 'Exclusive Confession of Dr Death's Mistress'. Pamela Collison's 'own version of her bizarre affair with Paul Vickers, the surgeon who murdered his wife' began with a sick joke invented by 'the mistress in the poison and passion trial' herself — 'I kissed the frog, but instead of a prince he turned into a poisoner.'

The *News of the World* paid Miss Collison £50,000 for her story and only the November circulation figures will show whether the investment has, at least, increased the paper's readership. Mr Askew, having asserted (with straight face) that it is 'very much in the public interest for people to know that there is a process of disguised poisoning by which you can be murdered called CCNU,' went on, disarmingly, to add that he did business with Miss Collison because he 'felt it would sell copies of my paper.' He obviously thinks that he did a good commercial deal, though hardly one which compares with the agreement he made with Sonia Sutcliffe. The wife of the Yorkshire Ripper talked to the *News of the World* 'without a penny being paid'.

Mr Askew is very proud of the way he captured Miss Collison and of the skill with which his reporters rushed her story into the paper. No two accounts of how the deal was done agree with each other — the inevitable aftermath of the subterfuge that surrounded the negotiations. The boast that the *News of the World* triumphed by 'working harder and being cleverer' than the competition is, at least, partly true. But the paper was also lucky. One of its staff had a distant — but as it turned out, influential — acquaintance with a Collison confidante. And, most important of all, the paper had money. With its foot in the door and its hand full of pound notes the *News of the World* probably spent £20,000 it could have saved.

Its first bid was £95,000, made in the hope that Miss Collison's story would turn into a major national — perhaps international — scandal. It was offered on the understanding that payment would only be made if the information provided by 'Pamela, 35 (still in a state of shock after her five weeks trial)' came down to the *News of the World's* expectations. When it turned out that all she had to offer was the trash that eventually appeared, the bid was lowered to £30,000; a certain payment promised for whatever inconsequential details she was prepared to dredge up and spew out.

Bids were made to Miss Collison through her solicitor, Clive McKeog, who is properly professionally reticent about the whole business. On the morning of Saturday, November 22nd, just as the *News of the World* thought that the deal was about to be done, Miss Collison drew back. Some of the negotiators believed (or claim they believed), heard (or claimed they heard) that the *Daily Express* had made an offer of £40,000. Christopher Ward, the *Express's* recently appointed editor, denies outright (and with all the sounds of genuine outrage) that he even contemplated buying the story of a woman for whom 'his readers would have had no sympathy'. He had, however, heard rumours of other papers pretending interest, in the hope of adding a pound or two to the price paid by 'Britain's Biggest Selling Newspaper'. With copy-time approaching fast and fears about their rivals growing, the *News of the World* offered an unconditional £50,000.

Fiona McDonald-Hull of the London office and David Leslie, the paper's man in the north-east, moved from the Dragonara Hotel in Middlesbrough to a spot that Mr McKeog assured them was three minutes away from their quarry, a phone box just around the corner from the Royal County Hotel, Durham. Whatever the reason for the delay, the reporters waited impatiently from ten to three until twenty to four, phoning McKeog every ten minutes. Then they were told that Miss Collison had agreed and that Stuart Kuttner, an Assistant Editor, had made out and handed over one of his own cheques. McKeog left for what was left of Newcastle United's match at St James's Park. At ten minutes to four Fiona McDonald-Hull entered the hotel and met Pamela Collison for the first time.

At this point in the story it is impossible for any member of the NUJ not to begin to feel admiration for what subsequently happened. Miss McDonald-Hull told Miss Collison to start talking and only stop if she was interrupted. At five minutes past four David Leslie dictated the pre-written introductory paragraphs to the *News of the World* copytakers. From then on he took turns with Miss McDonald-Hull to keep the story flowing in, until the first episode of the sickening saga filled the front page and spilled over into the inside of the paper. Next morning, observing her handiwork, Miss McDonald-Hull had only one emotion. She was delighted that it 'read so well' and 'went in just as we dictated it'. As Ernest Hemingway almost said to Scott Fitzgerald, 'Anyone who can do anything so bad as that so well, ought to be doing something better.'

Jameson Raid

IT SEEMS TO me that Barry Askew has been badly treated.
That is, I am sure, a minority opinion. But neither the
evidence concerning his dismissal nor the rumours surrounding his sacking allow any other conclusion. Mr Askew was,
lovers of literary excellence will recall, plucked out of the
obscurity which is Preston and made editor of the *News of the
World.* But they are not long, the days of massage parlours.
And after eight months he was sacked. True, he maintained
the traditions of 'Britain's biggest selling paper': he made an
excuse and left. But the resignation was as genuine as the
paper's claim to be 'as British as roast beef'. Rupert
Murdoch decided that a change was needed. So Mr Askew
was out of what he proudly called 'the chair' in less time than
it takes to jam an investigative foot in an errant curate's
door.

During his brief glory Mr Askew presided over at least a
numerical renaissance of the *News of the World.* There are
many reasons why — during his stewardship — circulation
stopped falling and began to rise. The new colour magazine
attracted new readers. So did bingo, that very present help in
time of newspaper trouble. The stridently pro-Thatcher line
was softened and a constant irritant to the paper's pre-
dominantly working-class readership was removed. It can be
argued that Askew was directly responsible for none of those
contributions to sales and solvency. But if he had presided
over a falling circulation, there can be no doubt who would
have been blamed. His successor, despite describing the
reason for his own appointment as 'if you want circulation,
send for Jameson', willingly agrees that sales have risen
dramatically during the last six months' and describes his initial task as 'making sure we don't go backwards'. Murdoch
and Co have shown no such generosity.

Admittedly, Mr Askew did nothing to improve the tone of
the paper. He did not make it a Sunday replica of the
Financial Times, nor did he increase the book review section
or employ a fine art critic. But there is little evidence to
suggest that he was recruited with the idea of those specific
changes in mind. He was supposed to be rough and tough.
And rough and tough he was — 'with advantages', as Henry V

136

would have said had he been a *News of the World* reader. There was also a problem with one of Prince Hal's descendants. For it was said — mostly by rival editors who enjoyed the story immensely — that Mr Askew made a fool of himself in front of the Queen.

The occasion was the meeting at which Fleet Street editors responded to the invitation to discuss the intrusive attention that was being lavished on the Princess of Wales by Press photographers. Mr Askew proposed that when the cameramen's devotion became intolerable, the young Princess send out a servant to buy the wine gums to which, apparently, she is addicted — an idea described by the Queen as the 'most pompous suggestion' that she had ever heard. Loyalty prevents a careful contextual analysis of Her Majesty's wounding thrust. So we cannot even consider if 'pompous' was really quite the right word. Nor can we speculate about whether the wine gum rule is applied in the Royal Household when convenience would best be served by enlisting a butler, footman or maid, rather than doing the job Oneself. We must however applaud the quality of the Royal Repartee. But if the unhappy Mr Askew was penalised for falling victim to an example of Her Majesty's one-liners, all our definitions of how absurd pomposity can become will need revision — it seems unlikely that Mr Murdoch bothered himself with such metaphysical questions. All he wanted was an editor who would cut a better figure at Court.

According to popular legend, the candidate he appointed is not the smoothest man in London. Indeed, he has the reputation for being the hairiest man since Esau. But lest a second confrontation is planned between Monarch and Fourth Estate, let me reassure the quaking Lord Chamberlain, Derek Jameson is not Sid Yobbo of *Private Eye,* the whelk-weaned Cockney who shuffled his way to fame and fortune down the refuse-littered Mile End Road. Of course, he has funny teeth, a funny voice and a couple of other characteristics which encourage Richard Ingrams and the other chaps from the Shrewsbury Lower School to give him a hard time. But he is a far more complex character than either Lord Gnome's employees, or the papers that have accepted their judgement, pretend.

He really does mind the Sid Yobbo label. It is not wholly

admirable to say out loud, 'If you come from the bottom and reach the very top and all they call you is a yobbo, it hurts.' But if it represents active expression of feeling, it betrays either a sensitivity or a sentimentality that Mr Jameson does not only exhibit on his numerous television chat show appearances. I actually believe him, and I rejoice at the discovery. A Fleet Street editor who feels that he is being badly treated by Fleet Street is an unexpected blessing, It provides more pleasure than simple joy at biter bit. It offers a tiny prospect of improvement in one paper.

For fate has suddenly provided Derek Jameson with a chance to prove his critics wrong. He has taken charge of a fundamentally nasty paper which exploits the seamy side of life and is regularly willing to ruin some nonentity's life rather than miss the publication of a single salacious paragraph. Sid Yobbo would just continue to run the same old sordid paper, without even remembering that the Yorkshire Ripper revelations and the Doctor Death story did not save his predecessor. A different man — particularly one with the self-confidence that Jameson appears to exude — would fight the circulation war by making the *News of the World* a better paper. Derek, it is up to you.

Death Wish

LAST WEEK THE prurience that always bubbles just below the surface of Britain's popular press broke out in a most unpleasant rash. The attack of ethical eczema was brought on by the current crime and punishment controversy. But its underlying cause was the cheaper papers' least attractive affliction — the desire to moralize and titillate at the same time. The passion to be simultaneously salacious and sanctimonious breaks out in the most virulent form on Sundays. Give the *News of the World* a really unwholesome story and it will salivate and sermonize at the same time.

But last week it was almost beaten into second place in the humbug competition. The *Sunday People* — which usually lives up to its boast of being the all-family paper — had two

138

items in nauseating juxtaposition. On page ten it published a genuinely uplifting, but palpably ignorant, leader. After a brief flirtation with penal populism ('terrifying sentences . . . for those who commit terrifying crimes') it defended 'those MPs . . . who rightly refuse to bring back the rope' when 'Parliament debates hanging . . . this week'. No such debate was to take place. But if the mention of that imminent Parliamentary occasion had been the only error, the mistake would not have mattered. However, the subject was pursued on page four.

There, next to 'Oo-la-la! He's the Pasty Pin-up' was a description of how 'Retired judge Sir Melford Stevenson . . . revealed a twenty-five-year-old secret'. Apparently the gentleman in question arranged for Ruth Ellis, 'the last woman to be hanged in Britain', to have a 'blonde rinse in Holloway prison, so that she could look her best when she appeared for sentencing at the Old Bailey. "Poor dear, I will never forget her," sighed the 79-year-old High Court judge.' Neither will the popular papers. Blonde, young, promiscuous and hanged by the neck until dead, her memory will stay green and profitable in all of Fleet Street.

The *News of the World* has certainly not forgotten her. They dredged up Georgina Ellis dressed to look like her executed mother, 'a bubbly blonde in the Marilyn Monroe mould'. Although 'professional model' Georgina insisted that 'I never dwell upon her death', she managed to break through her inhibition for long enough to call for the return of the death penalty. Her carefully considered criminological judgement was part of a feature on the subject of judicial execution that was spread across pages six and seven.

Naturally enough, 'Bring Back the Rope' (complete with an artist's impression of the way in which the condemned man's legs are pinioned in preparation for the big drop) was provided as a public service. 'Today,' the feature began, 'the *News of the World* focuses on an issue that has set all Britain talking.' The national conversation which was afforded most prominence involved reporter Alan Hart and 'Britain's official hangman, Harry Allen'. The prematurely superannuated public servant announced that he was 'ready and willing to go back to work'.

But Mr Allen is not a man without feeling. Although he has

'never felt a moment's remorse' during his working life, he clearly approached his work with real compassion.

'I've seen various methods of execution,' be explained, 'and I'm convinced that the noose is the most humane. It takes no more than eleven seconds — perhaps less — for the murderer to die once I've sprung the trapdoor.' Under the drawing of Mr Allen placing a noose around the hooded head of the condemned man was a caption that pointed out, with macabre absurdity, that 'the hangman wears a lounge suit'.

Naturally enough, Mr Allen is an unwavering supporter of capital punishment who 'blames the well meaning do-gooders for the mess that society is in today'. His vested interest in that point of view is obvious enough. It is not so much that he needs the work as that he needs the moral certainty that the men he has executed have not died in vain. How else could he honestly boast that his sleep is never disturbed by remorse or doubt?

In the *Sunday Express,* George Gardiner MP also called for the return of the death penalty. Mr Gardiner clearly believes in both hanging murderers and strangling the English language. He is devoted to the single-sentence paragraph, the conversational aside and Margaret Thatcher. His feature page article staggers from 'We have got to question the old assumptions, since it is clear we have been following totally the wrong track in dealing with criminals whether petty or big-time' through 'Alas, no' to a heavy type passage about his heroine in which SHE is printed in capitals. Mr Gardiner does not have Harry Allen's literary ability but he fits exactly into the strident populism of the *Sunday Express* leader page.

If the *Sunday Express,* the *People* and the *News of the World* made the right judgement about what their readers wanted, the *Sunday Mirror* took a considerable risk in standing out against the cry that violence should be met with violence. For a popular Sunday paper to print a leader headlined 'Too much fuss from the fuzz' is, at any time, an act of considerable courage. To ask 'Isn't it about time the police stopped whingeing and got on with the job' in a week when its rivals were using the death of two young policemen as evidence in favour of the introduction of Draconian laws, was brave to the point of recklessness.

It may, however, turn out in the end that the *Sunday Mirror* was shrewd as well as rational. Too often (for their circulation as well as reputation) the *Sunday Express* and the *News of the World* underestimate their readers. It is not only Balliol men (like Mr Gardiner) who are likely to be nauseated by the hangman's testimony and the Ellis disinterment. And it may even be that some people, reading the Gardiner column as they listened to the Morning Service on the radio, actually heard the answer to his question, 'Why should a policeman die and his killer's life be saved?'

Mail Disorder

ACCORDING TO THE television advertisement, the demand for *Mail on Sunday* still exceeds supply. Even in Week Three — when at least Christopher Fildes felt sufficiently secure to drop the eighteen-word explanation for his appearance in the paper — the newsagents were said to have sold out. Fildes felt confident enough to call himself plain 'city editor' rather than 'former financial editor of the *Daily Mail,* city editor of the *Spectator,* the *Evening News* and founder editor of *Euromoney'.* But readers were still bubbling with as much excitement as if the *Mail on Sunday* had just been launched. Or so we are assured.

If the claims are anything like true, *Mail on Sunday* readers bubble easily. For, far from providing something new to fill a long-felt week-end want, Lord Rothermere's 'haughty but naughty' new newspaper looked tired and shopsoiled from the start.

Take, for example, the main attraction of the inaugural issue. Jilly Cooper's article on 'Whimps' would have won a prize in a Women's Institute 'Satirize Jilly Cooper Contest'. But it is hardly surprising that when it was submitted to the *Sunday Times,* the fastidious brahmins of Grays Inn Road did not print it. The *Mail on Sunday* got it secondhand.

In so far as I understand Miss Cooper's article, it was a demand for the return of the dominant masculine male. But

141

her real enthusiasm for the 'heterosexual middle aged' man who 'rules the roost like Chanticleer' seems open to some question. Rejected by Frank Giles and the macho monsters of the *Sunday Times,* she did not kiss the lash. Instead she flounced off to the Shrimsley brothers who seem willing to accept whatever quality of favour she is ready to bestow.

Shrimsley Junior (complete with a picture that is meant to look like Rodin's *Thinker* if the model had been a snappy dresser, but which only succeeds in conveying the impression of a man wriggling his finger in a wax-obstructed ear) is clearly destined to become the *Mail on Sunday's* star political columnist.

Like Hannibal he requires no description other than his name. If only he had felt, like Christopher Fildes, that an explanation was necessary, his by-line might have proved a connoisseur's item amongst copy writers — 'resident Harold Wilson apologist of the *Sunday Mirror,* founder and liquidation editor of *Now!,* brother of the editor.'

In the first issue of *Mail on Sunday,* Mr Shrimsley (Junior) was denied the leader page in favour of Brian Walden, though the editorial itself, headed 'A leader with the touch of Churchill', had all the hallmarks of his elder brother during his high *News of the World* period. Mr Walden's article must have delighted the paper's more nostalgic readers.

It was a profile cum attack upon Sir Keith Joseph, presented in the form of an imaginary conversation between Sherlock Holmes and Doctor Watson. It would not have won a prize in a 'Satirize Conan Doyle Competition'. The Baker Street Dialogue has been the refuge of overstretched journalists for over seventy years. The extraordinary thing, my dear Watson, is that such a pastiche should be the centrepiece of the first edition of a new paper.

But then, the *Mail on Sunday* clearly has the courage to imitate. The confessions of Billie Jean King combined prurience and priggishness in proportions that were reminiscent of the old *Empire News.* 'If I had been caught making love to a male movie star at high noon in Times Square, it wouldn't even make the six o'clock news. But Billie Jean and a woman . . .' Salivate as you sympathize. Preach your sermon from the respectable side of the keyhole. All human humbug is there.

And the *News of the World* overtones are even more pronounced in what passes for news stories. 'Scandal of Animal Smuggling Racket', like 'Wife who Escaped the Double Killer' and 'Love was the Only reason says Peer's Daughter who Married the Man from the Heavenly Sect', is a headline reminiscent of another age. When I saw 'Tragic Beauty's Last Hours' I began to suspect that the sub-editors were doing it on purpose and that the next set of TV commercials would invite us down Memory Lane.

To complete the illusion, there was a double-page spread of film-star confessions appearing in successive weeks under the title 'Loving and Losing Elizabeth'. The Elizabeth in question was of course Mrs Hilton, Mrs Wilding, Mrs Todd, Mrs Fisher, Mrs Burton, Mrs Burton and Mrs Warner. In Week Three of the 'new' *Mail on Sunday,* there was an 'exclusive preview' of Eddie Fisher's psychological problems. 'My ego couldn't have asked for anything more. I had rejected Elizabeth Taylor.' In Week Four the *Mail on Sunday* moved further back in time and described the Michael Wilding years.

To do the *Mail on Sunday* justice, the recruitment of John Osborne to write 'Looking Back' (a sort of generalized criticism of the previous week's television) is something of a coup. But Mr Osborne — not I suspect one of the *Mail's* favourite writers when he looked back angrily at the failures and foibles of the Establishment — produces pieces which show every sign of being extemporized into a dictating machine. In the contrived introduction to his review of *Play for Tomorrow* he concluded an obliquely relevant reference to the modern generation's ignorance of *Roses of Picardy* with: 'Flanders Fields? So bleats the lumpen sensibility of poxed populi.' That is, of course, just Jean Rook moved up market.

But then that is the *best* that can be said about the *Mail on Sunday.* The worst is perfectly exemplified by the first page of 'Lifestyle — eight pages of life plus style', on May 16th. 'International high lifer and columnist' Taki Theodoracopulos headed his column 'He who has a yacht has a different wife every night'. The idea that boat ownership was a sure way to sexual success was first brought to my attention by an article in the *Spectator* a few months ago. The author was called Taki — pronounced, I have no doubt, as in the colloquialism for cheap and nasty.

Secondhand as well as second-rate. Is that really what the southern suburbs have been waiting for ?

Lobby

Terms

Rogues' Gallery

FOR OVER THREE years I drove from Sheffield to Birmingham almost every Sunday morning, in order to work in the Parliamentary constituency which I hoped soon to call my own. I left home long before the papers were delivered, so I spent the first few miles of my journey anxiously peering through the North Derbyshire mist as I searched for an early-rising newsagent and a copy of the *Observer*. I rarely waited until I left the shop before I nervously turned to page two.

I actually expected to find buried in the political column the answers to my apprehensive questions about the prospects for Labour in general and the prospective candidate for Sparkbrook in particular. It never struck me that the three hours I was about to spend knocking on doors and canvassing opinions would provide a better guide to my future than the opinions of a lady who tapped away at a London typewriter. I was in thrall to Nora Beloff.

My unreasonable respect for political journalists persisted for over a decade. In 1970, sitting in a loudspeaker van outside the Lucas Battery Works, I was initially depressed that not a single employee had turned out for my eve-of-poll 'factory-gate meeting'. Rude signs from passing pedestrians did little to revive my spirits. But Robert Carvel of the *Evening Standard* did. 'This morning,' he told radio listeners, 'I saw Edward Heath fighting for the soul of his party in defeat.' Ignore the opinion polls, he urged, Labour is home and dry. Despite the angry housewives beating on the windscreen I believed him, right up to the moment the result was declared.

It was Mr Carvel who caused me finally to lapse from true faith in political commentators. I spent the summer of 1973 canvassing in the marginal constituencies of comrades and friends. Convinced that the time was right for an election, I composed a careful letter to the Prime Minister, arguing the irresistible case for dissolving Parliament. On the day that the letter arrived in 10 Downing Street, the *Evening Standard* headline screamed: 'The Fearful Five'. Mr Carvel's story listed me amongst the quaking quintet which was urging the Prime Minister to stay on. My inclusion was not even justified on grounds of style. 'The Fearful Four' has the same alliterative effect.

Mr Carvel cannot, however, claim first prize in the factual error competition. That award goes to Ronald Butt of *The Times*. In an article which implied that the Tribune Group was a species of political Triffid and about to engulf civilization, he gave an example of the feeble resistance to their ectoplasmic onrush. Even the Prime Minister, his horrified readers learned, had chosen to join rather than fight. Mr Butt had discovered the name Jim Callaghan on a list of Tribune members.

Unfortunately for Mr Butt, it was not the First Lord of the Treasury. The new recruit was Jim Callaghan, amiable art teacher and MP for Middleton and Prestwich. Mr Butt had not bothered to ask. The Prime Minister's reply to questions concerning his membership of the Tribune Group would have been easily understood. Similarly, I would have gladly revealed my view on the most desirable election date. Indeed, the best columns I read are those that bear the mark of my frank opinion.

Because he failed to make a simple phone call, Mr Butt stood convicted of a crime more serious than the confusion of two names. He was guilty of absurdity. Leonard James Callaghan was always the solitary reaper of political harvest — unwilling to join a Christmas Club in case it committed him to views he did not hold. Imagining that he joined the Tribune Group is so gross an error that it can only be explained by the excitement the apparent discovery caused. Mr Butt's enthusiasm for his argument temporarily incapacitated him.

There is nothing wrong with political journalists holding strong opinions. But the examples with which they illustrate their prejudices ought to have some bearing on the facts. And there ought to be no pretence of fair-mindedness. To his credit, Mr Butt lays no claim to objectivity. Unfortunately, the same cannot be said of all columnists. the *Guardian's* Peter Jenkins, writing of the Liberal/Social Democrat pact, agreed that 'It is impossible to know exactly how the alliance will work,' but judged that 'its overpowering logic and natural momentum will overcome the local opposition.' He did not make clear that its chic charms had overcome him already.

The real problem with political columnists is that they are

often so busy putting the world (and politics) to rights that they have no time for the details. There are of course, commentators of great distinction — most of whom I dare not mention for fear they feel corrupted by my compliments. However, I can nominate John Cole of the *Observer* who, since he will soon join the BBC, is about to transcend all worldly temptations. Equally, Hugo Young of the *Sunday Times* writes a column of such consciously high-minded rectitude that no one would suggest he could be influnced by either praise or blame.

The political writers for politicians to watch and for everyone to respect are the real reporters. They may glory n the title of editor or correspondent, but they spend their time discovering and describing what is going on. Stanley Sparks of the *Birmingham Mail* and John Dickinson of the *Evening News* actually announced Alec Douglas Home's resignation from his Party's Leadership the day before it happened. They shared an office. And I have never been sure which one found out and which one was lucky. So I treated them both with great caution. It is the journalist who seeks information rather than the pundit who knows all the answers that politicians should fear.

Unbalancing the Budget

FOR FLEET STREET Budget week begins on Sunday with the annual competition to publish the silliest picture of the Chancellor of the Exchequer. In 1982 the *Observer* was the outright and undisputed winner, with a photograph of Sir Geoffrey and Lady Howe peeping through a Surrey windmill's window as if they were a pair of mechanical cuckoos waiting to pop out of the clock the moment that the hour struck. On Budget day itself, the cameras clicked for the usual cliches — Mr Gladstone's dilapidated despatch box held half aloft and a casual stroll amongst the snowdrops in St James's Park. Lady Howe — who misses far fewer tricks than her husband — came out on to the steps of No.11 with her own Instamatic. Picture editors find pictures of people taking pictures irresistibly attractive. So the Chancellor's wife 'snapping Downing Street photographers' appeared in the *Guardian*, the *Express* and provincial papers.

The national dailies' judgement of the Budget was made clear by their by-lines. In the *Daily Mail*, the *Guardian*, the *Express*, the *Star* and the *Mirror*, the front page lead was handed over to the political editors, who interpreted the Chancellor's statement less in terms of national recovery than in the language of political survival. Terry Lancaster in the *Mirror* put the point more colourfully than his colleagues, but he echoed their general judgement. 'The Chancellor sipped gin and tried to give his party a tonic,' his story began. Mr Lancaster is not the man to waste a good metaphor, so he ended with 'It's true that the Budget pushed up the price of spirits — but it pushed up Tory spirits too.'

Of course, the *Financial Times* took the whole thing much more seriously and led with a sober list of the Budget ingredients written by its Economic Correspondent. As if to emphasize the objectivity of *Daily Telegraph* news stories, that paper's front page was dominated by a detailed description of the Chancellor's proposals that bore no prejudicial author's name. The *Morning Star* splashed a similarly anonymous table of Budget contents. But the '*Morning Star* reporter' who prepared the indictment would be deeply offended by the allegation of fairmindedness. 'Chancellor Sir Geoffrey Howe announced a budget for the bosses yesterday. In a one and three-quarter-hour rambling speech . . . ' The trouble with such obvious prejudice is that sensible people are reluctant to believe the facts behind the fulmination even when true.

In fact, the Commons 'Sketch Writers' — those extraordinary parliamentary critics who review debates as if they were plays and treat every afternoon as if it were a first night — came to a general agreement that Sir Geoffrey's speech was 'better and more competently delivered than in his previous Budgets'. That *Times* judgement was qualified by the *Guardian's* Michael White — undoubtedly the best of the cruel crew because he is both genuinely funny and free from the strange compulsion to be unpleasant about everybody all the time. According to him, one of the causes of the Chancellor's successful performance was the way in which he 'sandbagged' Opposition MPs into 'comatose acquiescence'. But then 'Sketch Writers' like to exude the weary superiority that comes from having heard it all before.

Michael White actually reminded his readers that, in a sense, that was literally true of the Chancellor's speech. 'The wonders of information technology,' he wrote, 'make it possible these days for the Budget statement to be delivered through the letter-boxes of AB newspaper readers on the Sunday before what is popularly known as Budget day.' Thanks to the Treasury's nods and winks, the posh papers were able to predict at least the shape and size of the Chancellor's proposals. For newspapers, that special boon ought to have been used to add extra hours to the time taken to prepare a considered comment. Clearly, not all of them used it in that way. Although the *Daily Star's* MUGGED! HOWE'S SMASH AND GRAB BODY BLOW warmed the cockles of partisans' hearts, the headline bore few signs of careful consideration or meticulous construction.

In the *Daily Star* — marvellously brash and wonderfully brazen — such excesses are both expected and welcome. Serious papers, however, ought to write seriously about major events. But as the Budget reports show, in journalism silly superficialities appear in many forms. Sometimes they are simply the product of prejudice. 'Something for everyone in the recovery Budget,' trumpeted the *Daily Mail*. FIRST STAGE TO LIFT OFF the big black headline continued. David English and Co have hoped for so long that 'the worst is over — official', that only the hardest-hearted critic would complain that they had taken the venerable comment out of cold store. The fact that it was inappropriate is neither here nor there.

But what of Peter Jenkins, the *Guardian's* 'award-winning columnist' who returned to his page in that paper a couple of weeks ago with a long confession of his own (and various infuriated colleagues') political associations? Most of Mr Jenkin's post-Budget column could have been written on the strength of last Sunday's news. Generality followed generality. The Prime Minister 'Hopes also to go into the election with her convictions intact saying "I held firm and, see, things are getting better" . . . For election-winning what matters is not who screams and applauds in the garages or pubs this week but what happens to the real economy in eighteen months' time.' A more vulgar paper might call the column 'So What's New?'

Mr Jenkin's final revelation concerned the all-important reaction of the Tory Party — in general terms that is. 'If interest rates don't come down while unemployment continues to rise, and if Mr Roy Jenkins wins at Hillhead and the Tories are routed in the Local Government elections, the temper on the backbenches could rise again.' The conditional 'could' is no doubt a reflection of Mr Jenkin's desire to avoid anything incriminatingly emphatic. The rest of the political pundits were sure that the Tory backbenchers had lost patience with political sacrifice and constituency unpopularity. The consensus was that the Budget was primarily intended to bring those dark days to an end. As to whether that objective would be fulfilled they were divided — not according to careful judgement but political prejudice.

Centre Court

IN COMMON WITH other members of my party, I have always believed that the Social Democrats owe at least part of their popularity to the affectionate coverage lavished upon them by what is popularly called 'the media'. Of course, like the Nile, the SDP has so many tributaries that its origins cannot be traced to a single source. Its creation owes a little to the changing nature of society, a lot to the self-destructive habits of the Labour Party and an incalculable amount to the habits and ambitions of its founding fathers — the founding mother riding the fiery chariot more as passenger than driver. But no one really doubts that newspapers and television helped the SDP's development.

Poor Bruce Douglas-Mann (the once but not future MP for Mitcham and Morden who resigned his seat when he left Labour for the SDP) actually complained on television that he had not received the coverage that candidates from the party had come to expect. The election of Roy Jenkins as mould breaker in chief provides an opportunity to examine the nature of Fleet Street's infatuation. With a handful of exceptions, it is not the result of journalists' personal commitment to SDP policies. The Social Democrats possess a quality which newspapers find irresistible. It is new.

Fleet Street loves novelty — pregnant pandas, space shuttles, race-riots, progressive Chief Constables, ra-ra skirts, deviant bishops, sex-change sailors and little girls who insist on playing centre-forward in their primary school football teams. For newspapers, the advertising slogan 'it's new and it's exciting' wastes three words. In most journalists' minds the two conditions are indivisible. The SDP was different and therefore it was news. Even the supermarket from which Bill Rodgers bought an unappetizing lunch for David Steel became a matter of gossip column interest.

Roy Jenkins, so long the darling of posh Sundays, thick weeklies and expensive dailies, got caught in Fleet Street's anti-time machine. Whatever other gifts Mr Jenkins possesses, he does not enjoy the attributes of a young outsider battling against the odds. The sudden enthusiasm for Dr David Owen sprang from the hope that the panda would really give birth and the Bishop would be caught in the act. One SDP-supporting correspondent whom I asked about his choice of leader had no doubt about his preference — 'Owen. That makes a far better story.'

The *Observer* was, in its way, most badly afflicted by the urge for novelty. On the Sunday before the SDP ballot closed it published an opinion poll that a majority of Social Democrat *supporters* favoured Doctor Owen. For years serious and sensible papers like the *Observer* had warned Labour about the need to distinguish between the passions of its members and the preferences of its potential voters. But the copy surrounding the poll seemed to assume that what the supporters desired the members would provide. An Owen profile was actually prepared for publication on the Sunday that followed his victory. Fortunately, Edward Heath was rotten to Mrs Thatcher earlier in the week and provided a ready subject for the rush-job with which the "Apotheosis of David Owen" was replaced.

It is astonishing that Adam Raphael, the *Observer's* political correspondent, did not warn them about their folly. Raphael is a Jenkins man. By that I do not mean that he supports the

SDP leader in any improper way, but that he regards Mr Jenkins as the best leader that the centre has got or could have. He is in favour of Mr Jenkins in the way that Catholic priests are in favour of large families. His professional judgement tells him what is best for the institution on which he is employed to pontificate, but he does not involve himself in the operational details required to bring the recommended solution about.

However, no matter how objective its intention, the article which Mr Raphael wrote on the Sunday before the SDP election was so helpful to its subject's cause that it might have been written by a member of Mr Jenkin's family — or even a more devoted supporter, say Lord Harris of Greenwich. Indeed, a column based on the notion that the SDP (and perhaps the whole of civilization as we know it) would collapse if Mr Jenkins was defeated would have seemed absurd had it been written by an admitted devotee.

Its strength lay in the supposition that the judgement was objective. The *Times* front page picture showing Mr Jenkins coming into his kingdom revealed Mr Raphael by his side, grinning from ear to ear. I attributed his joy not to partisan pleasure but relief that civilization had been reprieved.

Other newspapers carried photographs of Mr Jenkins at the SDP women's rally with Ms Polly Toynbee of the *Guardian* by his side. Ms Toynbee is the most prominent of the *Guardian's* numerous Social Democrats and came out of the closet as soon as the new party was founded. She stood for election as an SDP candidate in the local election and spoke with such passion at the party's February conference that her colleague, Michael White, reported the result of the vote on equal rights as 'Women's page 183: Sports page 214.' Nobody doubts where Ms Toynbee stands. Read her column and you read the views of a paid-up SDP member. Nobody, in my view, can complain about that.

If we have a complaint about Mr Raphael, it is not that he is a covert member of the clan. Biased I believe him to be, but not towards the new party. He is prejudiced in favour of his own judgement. He was almost the first journalist to prophesy the emergence of a new centre party. He constantly (and often correctly), predicted the next twist in Labour's downward spiral. If the SDP does become a major force in

British politics, Mr Raphael will be entitled to remind all of Fleet Street that he scooped the news years ago. However, until that day he ought to resist the temptation of publishing premature evidence of his triumph.

Printer's Devil?

THIRTY-FIVE YEARS ago I was in thrall to Len Hutton, Clem Attlee and four girls from North Yorkshire. One of them lived round the corner in Vainor Road and the other three came from the Parsonage at Howarth. I was also fascinated by a group of writers whose work was published in two slim (indeed emaciated) volumes. The first was called *Essays by Modern Masters*. The second, adding originality to arrogance, bore the title *More Essays by Modern Masters*. I admired E.V. Lucas and Robert Lynd almost as much as I envied their skill. I remember only one of Hilaire Belloc's contributions to the two anthologies. It was called The Honest Man and the Devil.

One night, the Honest Man 'had the misfortune to wake . . . and see the Devil standing by his bedside.' His visitor was not the heroic Satan of Paradise Lost but a boringly predictable Old Nick who immediately propositioned his reluctant host with an offer of immortality. Exceeding peace had made the Honest Man as bold as Abu Ben Adam. So he told the Devil to go to hell. The Devil obliged but left the bedroom with the warning that 'if you have nothing to do with me, I will have nothing to do with you.' The Honest Man professed himself wholly satisfied.

The Honest Man usually dictated his letters into a machine and his secretary typed them up from tape. But after his meeting with the Devil, he found that the words he spoke into the microphone were not the words which the contraption recorded. Invitations were answered with predictions that 'I shall feel out of place amongst your friends, but I need not stop long.' Appeals were donated trivial sums as an alternative 'to wasting any more time on this matter'. I thought the Belloc essay immensely funny and forgot about it for almost thirty years.

But last night, I dreamed the Honest Man's dream. The Devil did not appear to me. He visited Printing House Square and made improper advances to the unimpeachable political staff of *The Times*. Naturally that triumphantly honest group of journalists told the Devil to take his offer of immortality elsewhere. But — as so often is the case in politics — virtue turned out not to be its own reward. The Devil said again 'I will have nothing to do with you.' And the next night the stories dictated to the *Times'* copy takers were strangely distorted during transmission. On July 28th only sub-editors' vigilance saved several distinguished careers.

Julian Haviland believed that he composed a story which began 'Friends of Mr Bernard Weatherall have satisfied themselves that unless some outstanding candidate comes forward he would have majority support to become Speaker if Mr George Thomas retires next year. There was much surprise,' Mr Haviland continued, 'at a newspaper report which said that Labour MPs and some Conservatives would not welcome his election ... ' But when it reached the newsdesk it had become 'A friend of Bernard Weatherall button-holed me in the Members Lobby. He was worried about propaganda put out by supporters of Weatherall's rivals for Speaker. But Weatherall is well liked and I think that I was at school with the man who cornered me'.

Anthony Bevins used to work for the *Daily Mail*. So he was not surprised to find that somebody had tampered with his story. He thought he had written that 'there is a significant number of Labour MPs who still believe that Michael Foot will indeed make the ultimate sacrifice after the October Party Conference.' But, changed by a diabolical hand, his article told a similar tale in a different way. 'Those hysterics waylaid me again last night. Normally, I hide behind statues of Gladstone when I see them approaching. But we are into the silly season and stories about plots against party leaders always excite the general public. In Harold Wilson's day we had one almost every week and they were all taken seriously by someone. In any case my column will probably appear under a thousand words from Ronald Butt, so by the time that readers get to me their minds will be a total blank.'

Ronald Butt found the Devil particularly difficult to handle.

156

At first, Mr Butt did not recognize his visitor, and simply assumed from his horns and forked tail that a member of the Labour Party National Executive Committee had come to call. When Mephistopheles identified himself there was still some confusion about his intentions — Mr Butt apparently believing that the Devil wanted to nationalize *The Times*. But once such errors were corrected, the senior pundit of Printing House Square started to write his article. He thought that he included a passage about the rules governing the immigration of English women's foreign husbands. 'For immigration to continue on any scale though such marriages would be politically unacceptable. So would a reversal by the Government... of its restrictions... whatever the European Human Rights Commission says about it.'

But it arrived in the feature editor's ofice in a rather different form. 'I have no idea how many English women are denied the right to live here with their husbands. But the number is not the point. I simply report a feeling in the Tory Party. They are against any more blacks living here. If the European Commission on Human Rights says that a few more should be let in, a problem arises. For the anti-immigration people made a great fuss of the Commission when it ruled against the closed shop. However, they will not allow the allegation of inconsistency to stand in the way of their prejudices.'

Hilaire Belloc's Honest Man was saved from the Devil's insistence on a surfeit of honesty by his secretary. Unfortunately, I woke up before I discovered how the Devil was defeated in Printing House Square and the smooth professional prose restored to its original state of bland grace. But I am happy to report that like Mr Belloc's suburban Faust each of the journalists 'saved his soul and at the same time his face which, if it were the less valuable of the two organs, was none the less of considerable moment to him.

Labour Pains

THE TRAIN ON which I travelled to Blackpool ran out of alcohol in Preston. It was also packed with journalists. I have no evidence to suggest that the two facts were directly related. But I can report that there was much to-ing and fro-ing between compartments and bar. For whenever a labour correspondent swayed past me (destabilized, I must explain, solely by the lateral movement of the carriage), I stopped him and asked a nervous question concerning the intentions of the Transport and General Workers' Union. Would the T & G delegations support Michael Foot's campaign against the Militant Tendency?

Of course, most journalists know less than I do about the working of this great party of ours — well, at least this great party of mine if not theirs. But like so many politicians, I cannot rid myself of the naive belief that news stories must have at least a nugget of truth buried under the dross of prejudice and ignorance, so I asked my neurotic question.

The *Daily Express* was certain and explicit. The Transport and General executive had decided to oppose the Foot formula for preventing infiltration. So the conference delegates would do the same. Fortunately (at least for those of us who think that the Labour Party needs Trotskyites like it needs an ice-pick in the head), the *Daily Express* was wrong.

And for the first three days of last week the papers persisted in their errors concerning the Labour Party Conference — often making mistakes by writing what they hoped would happen rather than reporting what the evidence suggested seemed probable. The dramatization began on Sunday when the *News of the World* led with a headline which announced, 'Back me or I go, says Foot.' The *Sunday Times* put the same point more colloquially with 'Foot: back me or I quit.' Cynics might suggest that the two reporters in question travelled to Blackpool together and discussed a rumour that had begun in Newcastle three days earlier, when the Labour Party Leader spoke at a meeting of the General and Municipal Workers' Union.

Other papers decided to dramatize Labour's struggle in a different way. To me, the decision of the National Union of Mineworkers to support the expulsion of Militant activists

158

meant another 236,000 votes towards the magic figure that produced a majority for action. John Fryer in the *Sunday Times* 'Foot quits' story did actually mention the numbers. Other correspondents concentrated on the personality. 'Militant — Miners No to Scargill' was the *Observer's* front page lead. 'Scargill gets a jolt,' the *Daily Express* whispered in a single inch of uncertainty whether to publicize defeat for one of its new ogres or victory for one of its old hate figures.

By Monday, Foot's victory was secure for, as the *Daily Telegraph* reported, 'The balance swung heavily against Militant when the Transport and General Workers' Union . . . reversed its earlier decison.' So the newspapers began to change the criteria of victory and defeat. Peter Jenkins in the *Guardian* announced that the 'purge would turn into the great Foot fudge', and the BBC used every bulletin to explain that the really significant pointer to Labour's new direction was not the Militant vote at all. A new hurdle had been created which the Labour Party had to climb if it was to win the establishment's seal of approval. What is loosely (and sometimes even pejoratively) called 'the Right' had to win extra seats on Labour's National Executive Committee.

The *Sun* stuck its neck out and predicted 'Mods set to grab power in the NEC', but other papers used their space to diminish the extent of Foot's success the previous day. 'Foot win fails to heal split', proclaimed the *Daily Telegraph* and followed up with 'Benn pledge to fight for Militant'. As a news item that story has all the novelty of dog bites man. But no doubt there was much rejoicing in the home counties at the reiteration of the obvious fact that the Labour Party had not become a monolith of blissful unity. All over Fleet Street, editors braced themselves for the bad news that the National Executive had swung to the Right and confirmation that the Party had voted twice in two days in a way which might actually increase its popularity.

To be fair, newspapers have not had much practice in constructing headlines like 'Labour swings Right — Foot gets power for purge', and all credit ought to be given to the *Daily Telegraph* for responding to the unusual situation with such bald clarity. Other papers were more politically ingenious. The *Daily Mail* could not resist 'Benn takes a beating.' But the *Daily Express* managed to do its duty by the Conservative Party with the headline (which occupied half its front page): 'Labour torn in half'. Newspaper readers with eclectic tastes could choose between fudging with Jenkins in the *Guardian* or splitting with John Warden, the Political Editor of 'The Voice of (Tory) Britain'.

The truth is that the media (to use an ugly but convenient word) have a substantial vested interest in a continuation of the muddle and mayhem within the Labour Party. Part of the enthusiasm is a result of political prejudice. But there is more to the enthusiasm for comradely chaos than the bias of a dozen press barons. Whilst the Labour Party was tearing itself to pieces it was theatre. And theatre excites journalists, as David Dimbleby demonstrated last Wednesday.

Just as the BBC came on the air an embarrassing announcement was made from the Labour Party platform. The scrutineers had miscalculated. At first it seemed that the Right-wing triumph in the National Executive elections was just the result of incompetent counting. But as the new figures were read out it became clear that the corrections made no difference to the political complexion of the NEC. The intonation of Mr Dimbleby's voice changed from elation to disappointment — not because he is politically prejudiced but because he is journalistically astute. What his sadness demonstrated is that a good week for the Labour Party is a bad week for the media.

Nott Answering

I AM BY nature a partisan person. So if someone had prophesied that John Nott might one day unfasten the microphone which was tearing a hole in his tie and stalk out of the *Nationwide* studio like an offended giraffe, I would have prayed for the prediction to come true. For the viewing public does not approve of that sort of thing. They expect politicians to take it on the chin, punch it out toe-to-toe or live out some other anatomical metaphor that keeps their posteriors firmly in the studio seat. Walking off displays either apprehension about what is to follow or distaste for what has gone before.

Cowardice in the face of Robin Day is a capital offence. So is condescension — at least as far as Sir Robin is concerned.

Now my dream of petty party advantage has come true. And I am still glad that Mr Nott made a minor spectacle of himself. But my reasons are rather different from those which I would have anticipated. Of course none of the Conservative Conference delegates who told him that he 'did exactly the right thing' really meant it. By behaving like an angry stick-insect the Secretary of State for Defence diminished himself and further lowered the level of popular esteem in which politicians are held. But he also struck a blow for sensible television interviews. I, at least, am prepared to sacrifice a small piece of Mr Nott's reputation to promote that cause.

There is, I know, great concern amongst the younger end of the BBC production staff about the way in which some of their current affairs programmes turn out. The political interview cannot sensibly be used as a star vehicle. It may well be that last week's little public *frisson* will liberate the critics who, for years, have only mumbled under their breath, and allow them to insist that politics on television should concentrate on the ideas and performance of the parties, not the character and personality of the interviewer.

Of course, I lay myself immediately open to the charge that I reflect nothing more than the opinion of the professional politician's trade union — an institution which would like to include in the BBC Charter a clause guaranteeing a soft ride for every politician who ever looks into a camera. In fact, quite the reverse is true. Sensible members of my profession do not mind being roughly handled. Being human, they may grow annoyed at being chivvied and chased from one half-sentence to the next. But they do not fear the constant interruption. There are all sorts of cheap popularity to be gained from both the soft answer that demonstrates composure and the quick retort that displays confidence.

Any politician who wrestled Robin Day to the studio floor would shoot up the popularity charts. And I myself was inundated with wholly unironic compliments on my compassion when (a fortnight ago on *Panorama*) I laid my hand on his be-knighted arm and urged him not to get upset. It is all good clean fun. The gladiatorial interview is the current affairs

161

equivalent of all-in wrestling.

There is a lot of action and nobody gets hurt. But nobody gets enlightened either. Jackie Pallo versus Big Daddy is simply cheap entertainment. Robin Day versus John Nott should be something more.

It should, ideally, be an opportunity for a politician's policies to be discussed and the weaknesses of both his plans and his personality to be exposed. And that — believe me — is best done by allowing the subject of the interview to finish the occasional sentence. It is, of course, harder work for the interviewer who has to prepare himself by mastering (say) the intricacies of the various nuclear options rather than by simply picking up gossip about a Minister's popularity or a party's divisions.

David Dimbleby does it. So does Gus Macdonald of Granada, John Tusa of *Newsnight* and, above all, Alastair Burnet of ITN. To elevate the sporting metaphor from wrestling to cricket: being interviewed by any of them is like batting against a remorseless fast bowler who always aims for the stumps. Bumper after bumper flying over the batsman's head neither intimidates the participant nor entertains the audience.

The kind of interview which politicians fear most is the kind that used to be conducted by Michael Charlton and Julian Haviland. Both of them were meticulously courteous. Neither of them ever raised his voice. But both persisted in calmly asking difficult questions. In my Ministerial days, when I was to be cross-examined by such formidable opponents, I always asked colleagues to prepare me for the ordeal by helping to anticipate the most difficult questions.

The suggestions which made me break out in a cold sweat and anticipate counterfeiting throat infection were the apparently soft options — the genuine request for information followed by a silence that had to be filled by my ignorance, the offer to allow me to clear up the impression of inconsistency, puzzled concern that one of my answers was factually wrong. I used to pray that they would cover my fumblings and mumblings with hectoring interruptions.

But I do not mean to discuss the techniques of television interviewing simply in terms of a politician's preferences. Television influences our attitudes towards serious matters no less than it develops our taste for Pot Noodles or Cup-a-Soup. So the worst sort of television interview has been a major force in the trivialization of politics. For it has created the false and fatuous impression that the world is too complicated to be governed in monosyllables is prevaricating. I know that last week in *Nationwide* John Nott did nothing for his own reputation. But I cannot help thinking that the wrong man left the studio.

By-Lines

WHEN I WAS fourteen, and clothed in the glorious raiment of youth club cricket captain, I prided myself on being the Norton League's most pragmatic field setter. Other infant skippers (who had watched the world's great bowlers spinning off breaks at Bramall Lane) always posted two of their juvenile contemporaries at backward short-leg to snatch up the catches which would surely come when the ball began to turn and the batsman chose to play it off his legs with the spin. The theory had three shortcomings. None of our bowlers could bowl an off-break. None of the opposing batsmen could glance the ball off his pads. And neither of the fielders could take the sharp half-chances which we had seen snapped up by Tony Lock and Johnny Wardle.

In fact, the impractical boy cricketers from other youth clubs did what they thought they were supposed to do rather than what seemed sensible in their own more modest circumstances. I am often reminded of those old concessions to convention when I attend by-election press conferences. Too often they amount to no more than highly talented candidates making statements which, if they are reported at all, only appear in journals which hardly any of their local electors read. In cities with local evening papers the press conference is a daily necessity. In the constituencies which boast a clutch of local periodicals it is just as important. But last week I was not at all surprised to see even John Spellar (in *Birmingham Mail* territory) and Harriet Harman (in south London's weekly paper belt) hurry on to more important duties before the last question had echoed out of their dusty committee rooms.

The assembled correspondents do little to encourage the feeling that something important is going one. At Ms Harman's initial campaign confrontation, the first question came from Guy Rais of the *Daily Telegraph* who asked if future press conferences could begin half an hour later. The timing of these occasions is complicated by the need for the Fourth Estate to move *en masse* between all of the candidates. If the confusion of conferences was the cause of Mr Rais's problem, he really should not have complained. For last week at the second Peckham press conference which I attended, he held his notebook in front of him like a policeman in the witness-box and read out, word for word, a 'challenge' which he had taken down in shorthand from the Conservative candidate's own lips. The long question and the short answer filled his column the following day.

Admirers of Bernard Shaw's *St Joan* will find the name of the *Telegraph's* man in south London vaguely familiar. That paper's more regular by-election correspondent, Godfrey Barker, also rejoices in literary associations. Together with Keith Raffan of the *Daily Express,* he regularly produces a performance which might reasonably be mistaken for a dramatic reading from the works of P. G. Wodehouse. Mr Barker — with well-cut tweeds when he ventures out of London and a smile which comes and goes without any apparent relationship to what is going on around him — is essentially Bertie Wooster. Mr Raffan — not quite a gentleman in double-breasted blazer and almost regimental tie —is Jeeves, but with a smaller vocabulary.

They both giggle a lot and give each other knowing looks. During the Beaconsfield campaign they were involved in an incident which scandalized their more assiduous colleagues. After one press conference a notebook and sealed envelope were found on or about the seats where they had been sitting. Anxious to discover the owner of these lost treasures, the Labour Agent first read the address on the brown manila. Its destination was "Vice-Chairman (Candidates), Conservative Central Office." Being a man of honour, he then decided to open the notebook. It was completely empty.

No one can be sure which, if either, of the Barker/Raffan

comedy duo had been so careless. But the evidence of the blank notebook is wholly consistent with its having belonged to Mr Raffan. Years ago, a Scottish Labour candidate described two of his helpers as his 'nanny' and his 'minder'. The descriptions were resuscitated in the spring election at Hillhead and they rose again from the dead in Coatbridge and Airdrie, where Tom Clarke (Labour's triumphantly local nominee) beautifully patronized his two supercilious 'visitors' from the sophisticated south by constantly thanking them for taking the trouble to come north and apologizing for the rigours of a brief sojourn in industrial Scotland. For reasons into which it is best not to enquire, the 'nanny' and 'minder' idea fascinated Mr Raffan and it constantly reappears in his by-election commentaries. Last week he was producing variations on the same theme from Peckham. But since only by-election devotees knew the origin of his obsession, the first half of his column had to be devoted to explaining what the second half was going to be about.

I do not mean to suggest that every journalistic participant in by-election press conferences chooses to trivialize what goes on as an alternative to working hard enough to understand the issues. Vincent Hanna of BBC's *Newsnight* often sits in a corner looking like the top half of one of the giants who gave Wotan such a hard time and, smiling, asks genially difficult questions. Last week in London, the *Guardian* sent a reporter called Susan Tirbutt who both enquired about the issues which were exercising Peckham electors and actually got the answers into the paper. But such seriousness is exceptional.

More typical is the tortuous reiteration of contrived hypotheses concerning personalities — who Ms Harman would have voted for had she been an MP during the election of Labour's deputy leader and which candidate for chairman of the Home Affairs Committee Mr Spellar would support if he were a member of the National Executive Committee. And the journalists invent their own rules of conduct and character. A candidate who declares the intention to talk about housing and unemployment, pensions and crime is considered to be evasive. If — God forbid — I ever become a by-election candidate, I would be extremely tempted to evade the press conferences altogether.

165

Court
and
Social

Engaging?

WHO CARES? The announcement that the Joint Parliamentary Under Secretary of State at the Foreign and Commonwealth Office gave lunch at Lancaster House last Monday for His Excellency The Roll of Congolium on the occasion of the Imperial Carpet and Floor Covering Exhibition can make few hearts beat faster in either Wigan or Wakefield. But such snippets of information do appear in our papers from time to time. Or at least in our papers from *Times* to *Telegraph*. For the market in Court and Social has been cornered by the top people's daily and by its bigger circulation rival which is not sure whether it aims at the Establishment or the hard-faced men who did well out of anything and everything.

Any other paper with space to spare and readers who retain a respectful interest in the institutions of the state could do exactly the same. When *The Times* published a full list of Royal Engagements for June, the twenty-four column melange was the result of assiduous collation by social Editor Margaret Alexander and her one assistant, who survived the recent staff purge. Had the idea appealed, the *Sun* could have done just the same by storing away the Press Association notices through which individual items in the Royal Programme are announced, and then printing the lot in majestic array. It could also record the eating habits of Junior Ministers. But since that is the one sort of trivia in which its readers are not interested (and neither the Palace nor the Foreign Office pay for space), such tit-bits are only recorded when the dinner ends in disorder or the lunch produces ptomaine poisoning.

In fact, the Buckingham Palace Press Office wishes that *The Times* would simply print the single facts of Royal Engagements on the day that the press notices are published. By hoarding them, in preparation for a pretentious omnibus presentation on mornings when there is a shortage of other news to fill its pages, *The Times* causes palpitations throughout the length of the land. Recipients of royal visits find it difficult to believe their good fortune until they have seen the news confirmed in print. And they are positively forbidden to brag about it before the official announcement is made. Until they read about it in the newspapers the tree-planting ceremony in the Bishop Berkeley Memorial Quad cannot exist.

Of course, an earlier proclamation may be promulgated in the attenuated rival column published by the *Daily Telegraph*. But that is not the same. That paper does not get its Nancy Mitfords quite right. It reports not 'social news' but 'events' — a word redolent of the Inner Wheel bring-and-buy sale. When it records a marriage it calls it a wedding. And it occasionally allows undesirable items to elbow their way into embarrassing proximity. 'Captive fox "was thrown to hounds" ' and 'Hatcher wins Bisley grand aggregate' pass muster. But 'Veteran coal-carrier, 66, decides to quit' carries an unpleasant suspicion of social confusion. Not simply Moss Bros at the reception but sometimes short jackets instead of tailcoats above the pin-stripe trousers.

And the 'forthcoming marriages' (both papers describe *future* nuptials correctly) are very important. They are the remunerative up-market end of the classified advertisement business — £5 a line in *The Times* and £6 a line in the *Telegraph*. Of course, some of the other little items also appear on the exalted pages as a result of money changing hands. Only one or two public schools (their identities easily guessed but officially kept a Printing House Square secret) have their Founder's Day recorded free of charge and their cricket captain's name announced for nothing. If you are the bursar of a minor Victorian foundation or the secretary of a trade association anxious to establish your place in society, you will have to pay for your moment of recognition in much the same way that a man in Sutton Coldfield with a secondhand car to sell pays when he phones 'Teleads' at the *Birmingham Mail*.

Some people actually choose double exposure of their nuptials — and discover as a result the positions that they occupy in the rival papers' tables of precedence. If your Dad is a Lieutenant-Colonel and your Mum a Lady, your engagement is likely to appear at, or near the top of, the list of those sharing your initial. Thus C. P. B. Freeman of that ilk (Buxhall Vale, Stowmarket, Suffolk) achieved principal billing in both *Times* and *Telegraph*. The decision is taken according to the rank and status of the male connection. If the pecking order was based on the distaff side his bride-to-be (Hilary Jane, youngest daughter of Mr and Mrs Henry Val Faker of Brentwood, Essex) would have ensured the couple's relegation to the second column.

Birthdays pose no precedence problem for either social page. In *The Times's* 'Birthdays Today', the alphabet is all. So the Baroness Wootton of Abinger CH appears at the foot of the column. The *Daily Telegraph* constructs 'Today's Birthdays' gerontologically, with Baroness Wootton coming second at 85. On the same day Sir John Gielgud appeared in both papers. But Rod Steiger and Julie Christie only rated a mention in *The Times*. However, Graham Greenwell (I assume *the* Graham Greenwell) made it in the *Telegraph* but not *The Times*. *The Times* even omitted mention of Viscountess Torrington who 'gave birth to a daughter at Winchester'.

But the real stars are, of course, the Orpen-Palmers, the Parsons-Smiths, the Montague-Evans, the Raw-Reeses, and the Doull-Connollys — all of whom announced weddings or marriages last week. S. J. Perelman used to buy his airmail edition of *The Times* principally for the pleasure of reading the names. And Paul Theroux found an edition in which Captain Sir Weldon Dalrymple-Champneys and Miss Inch both appeared. On the day of that discovery Sir Ranulph Twistleton-Wykeham-Fiennes reached the South Pole. He did the North Pole during the double-barrelled days of mid-April. Of course, the object of the social pages is to prove that whatever we hope and think, nothing changes very much.

Baby Bio

WHATEVER MAY BE happening in other parts of our sagging economy, one industry is undoubtedly booming. 'Lady Di has become a national treasure,' wrote the *Sunday Express*. And that paper ought to know. For 'as she awaits her baby', its colour magazine is publishing 'four exclusive extracts' from her 'first authoritative biography' written by Robert Lacey, 'the author of *Majesty,* the international bestseller about her mother-in-law, the Queen.'

Anyone who needs to be reminded of the relationship

between Diana Windsor and Elizabeth II could easily be confused by another part of the serial's description. The claim that it is the 'authoritative' biography may lead some sloppy readers to believe that it is 'authorized' — the prize for which all biographers of royalty (and their stockbrokers) yearn.

The claim to be 'authoritative' cannot be tested in court or against objective criteria. Readers must judge for themselves whether or not they are given an authentic glimpse of life inside the palace gates. Writers anxious to insinuate the impression of being 'in the know' insert a quick flash of intimate conversation only available to flies on walls and those who walk with kings but keep the commercial touch.

Thus, Mr Lacey reported that Lord Spencer told his daughter to 'marry the man you love' and that the blushing bride-to-be replied, 'That is what I am doing.' Presumably he was not present when the dialogue took place. The claim to have written an 'authoritative' biography would have been enhanced by a footnote giving the precise source of such an important piece of information.

Of course, I am not doubting Mr Lacey's word — just disapproving of a technique which is the constant refuge of royalty-watchers who have to pretend that they are royalty-overhearers as well. Audrey Whiting's 'Royal Baby Diary' in the *Sunday Mirror* played the same trick. Her first article was full of quotations. 'A close friend of the Royal Family' told her that 'the Queen was determined that the baby — destined to become Monarch if it was a boy — should be born under the Monarch's roof.'

On the evidence of the Court's anonymous Deep Throat, the *Mirror* claimed 'exclusive' credit for the revelation that there was 'considerable debate' within the Royal Family about the place in which the birth should happen. Miss Whiting is not a lady to suggest friction between monarch and heir apparent. Indeed, the Buckingham Palace supergrass reported that 'there was no heated argument'. But the suggestion that Prince Charles's preference for a London hospital had been overruled by the Queen was in fact the nearest she got to justifying the claim to exclusivity.

For the fact (if fact it is) that the baby is to be born 'at home' in the specially converted Buhl Room was central to the story that appeared in the *Sunday People* on the same day. It was headed 'world exclusive' for no better reason than that Bonnie Estridge ('author of the best-selling *Pregnancy — How to Look Good and Feel Good*') speculated in that paper alone about the composer of the music that would be piped into the delivery room to sooth Diana's nerves.

Miss Estridge also revealed that if the infant experiences a 'slight delay in breathing' the nurse 'may deliver an old-fashioned smack on the baby's bottom'. And as she has written a best-seller, the reader is expected to cherish such bits of fascinating information. In the *Sunday Express*, Mr Lacey demanded similar unquestioning respect as author of an 'international best-seller'. Readers who enjoy deferential articles are obviously susceptible to demands for literary defence.

The *Sunday Telegraph* also has an 'exclusive' series about the young Princess. Like the *Sunday Express* and the *Sunday People*, the *Telegraph* makes the claim because its chosen author appeared in no other paper. There is certainly nothing unique about most of the information in the extracts from Penny Junor's book. Inevitably she and Mr Lacey, recording the life of a twenty-year old lady, to whom nothing very eventful happened before her eighteenth birthday, are bound to produce similar stories. They have also produced identical reactions in other Sunday papers — panic.

For there can be little doubt that the *Sunday Mirror* and *Sunday People* cobbled together their own Princess Di stories in response to the news-stand appeal of the two 'exclusive' Royal biographies. It is the only possible explanation to the extraordinary lengths to which those papers went to say something — anything — about the young Princess. Consider, for instance, an item from Miss Whiting's second diary entry. 'A journalist who has seen the Princess at close quarters thinks that she is very sexy with a great figure.'

But that is not the best example of secondhand reporting that the Sundays provided. The *Sunday People's* main response to the threat from Lacey and Junor was brazenly frank about its derivative origins. Woman's Editor, Patricia Boxall, revealed 'The Many Sides of Princess Di' based on 'the many books and biographies written about our newest Royal — including Robert Lacey's *Princess*, Penny Junor's *Diana*,

173

Princess of Wales . . .'

The Royal baby is still two months away. And I have no doubt that we can look forward to more miracles of contrivance and additional excesses of invention all the way to its delivery in the Buhl Room. When it actually arrives the popular newspapers will be almost too preoccupied with the single subject to find room for the latest free publicity photograph of Joan Collins. They will all explain they they are simply giving their readers what they want — a real-life fairy story to lighten the darkness of a depressed world. But real-life fairy stories are supposed to be fantasy, not fiction. And if they are padded out by irrelevance and invention the magic disappears like Cinderellas's fine clothes at midnight.

Baby Talk

DEAR SIR WILLIAM REES-MOGG,

You really must abandon the habit of writing newspaper articles in the style of letters. It is a contrivance usually associated with desperation at deadline time and should be left to tyro-journalists who have space to fill but nothing to say. Tired old subjects are not reinvigorated by treating them as if they are personal messages to famous people — though readers are embarrassed by the obvious artifice.

You seem to specialize in writing letters to recipients who cannot read — a practice which emphasizes the artificiality of the whole technique. Fifteen years ago, you addressed your newly-born son through the,columns of a national newspaper. Last week you were pushing your ideas through the nursery letter-box again. I am not sure what your recent *Sunday Times* article was about. But it was dressed up to look like avuncular advice offered exclusively to the four-day-old Prince William of Wales.

I was prepared to excuse the letter to your son as the product of sudden sentimentality. Of course, commoners like you and me should regard a birth in the family as a matter for private rather than public rejoicing. But his father's abandonment of proper post-natal reticence does not seem to have permanently damaged Master Rees-Mogg. True, at the tenderest of years he made well-publicized appearances at company annual meetings and complained about the small dividends that were paid on his infant shares. But your neighbours tell me that he spent most of last summer practising his forward defensive stroke in the back-yard. A boy obsessed by cricket cannot have been totally ruined by his upbringing.

If your son is the prodigy that all who know his father must expect, I hope that he was not too severe about your letter to Prince William. I found the opening sentence particularly perplexing. Your article began with the assertion that 'No man can remember his own birth.' True, and no child of four days can read the *Sunday Times*. Of course, one day the Prince will be old enough to understand your article. But by then he will have forgotten his own birth and will regard your insistence that he cannot remember it as superfluous to the point of surrealism.

No doubt the Prince will be impressed by the way that you manage to be simultaneously deferential and patronizing in a single sentence. 'By the time that you come to study history, which no doubt one studies with a different type of interest when so much of national history is one's own family history . . .' is psychologically a most revealing passage. Though it teaches the next-king-but-one very little about prose style except the need to avoid prolixity. You do, however, go to some pains to instruct him in elementary history.

One passage of your letter reads, as you may recall,

'In the reign of Queen Elizabeth the First we defeated Philip II of Spain at the time of the Armada, under Queen Anne we defeated Louis XIV of France, under George III we defeated Napoleon, under George V we defeated the Kaiser's Germany and in the reign of George VI we defeated Hitler.'

Believe me, Sir William, I do not disagree with a word of that. Nor do I understand why you thought it worthy of publication on the front page of the *Sunday Times* Review.

At first I thought it was all leading to one of the conundrums of the sort that we are promised when we look in Joanna Southcott's box, and that you would disclose that all the listed monarchs were born on Wednesdays or had sailors for fathers or strawberry birthmarks on their left elbows. But no such revelation followed. The historical resume ended with a line which I suspect that you stole from E. J. Thribb. 'These were struggles on a very different scale — struggles of the world.' I think that the Thribb poem was called *In Praise of Bathos*.

The superficial reader may conclude that your letter was written in a spirit of romantic loyalty. But careful examination of the text suggests that you expect the future king to be an idiot. A normal boy will spend the early Nineties playing with silicon-chip-impelled Lego or some such scientific device. Only a blockhead will need to be reminded that 'in common with babies born in this or recent years' he will live in a world 'whose technology and science will be amazingly changed from what we know.' Normally, people are bored by being told what they already know.

They are also embarrassed by pomposity. And I therefore hope that William V will heartily dislike the prefabricated aphorisms with which his letter is littered. I give you only one example of your literary excess. 'Yours,' you actually told the future monarch, 'will be a Pilgrim's Progress, not because you were born royal, but because you were born human.' Sir William, as Chairman of the Arts Council and Deputy Chairman of the BBC, you really must resign from the Wayside Pulpit school of moral philosophy.

Indeed, you must do more. You must never write one of those bogus letters again. If you have anything to say, say it. If not, get out into the garden and bowl to that boy.

Yours sincerely,
Roy Hattersley

P.S. I am glad to see that you are still *persona grata* at Times Newspapers and that your likeness has not been painted out of old group photographs as if you were a disgraced Soviet general. De-Stalinization has overtaken your successor, Harry Evans. In Printing House Square it is as if he never was. Other papers marked his birthday in their lists of celebrity anniversaries. But the journal of record, which he used to edit, cut him out. You, Sir William, escaped just in time.

Knight Editor

IT IS THE Shrimsley brothers for whom I feel sorry. The Conservative Government's Patronage Secretary has now assembled six Conservative Honours Lists, yet they have not received a British Empire Medal between them. Bernard must fear that his years as editor of the *News of the World* — when sauna-bath exposés were interleaved with devotional items concerning the virtues of Mrs Thatcher — have been forgotten. And brother Anthony may suspect that his career has been sacrificed in vain. He allowed his by-line to appear over the *Sun's* most hysterically anti-Labour stories. Then he accepted the editorship of *Now!*, notwithstanding that magazine's obvious inability to survive. The Prime Minister attended the dinner that launched Sir John Goldsmith's most expensive baby. But although he was in charge of the loss leader, Tony never got a ribbon to stick on his coat.

If the Shrimsley siblings had an inclination towards literature, they would no doubt be filling the *Mail on Sunday* with quotations concerning winter winds being less unkind than Prime Ministerial ingratitude, and comparing a thankless Party Leader with a serpent's tooth. Since their proclivities lie in other directions, I suspect that they are more interested in the best way of explaining their lack of preferment to their friends. Last week, the task must have been particularly difficult. For last week, David English received a knighthood.

Some earlier unexpected awards could be dismissed as occasional aberrations. The elevation of Sir John Junor of the *Sunday Express* could be attributed to the Prime Minister's sentimental attachment to stories about Sunderland flying boats and 1950s-style layout. The accolade of Sir Larry Lamb of the *Sun* could be dismissed as a Saatchi and Saatchi contrivance intended to demonstrate that Mrs Thatcher was not too stuffy to approve of newspapers turning themselves into mail-order ladies' underwear catalogues. But now that David English of the *Mail* is to kneel before the monarch, the excuses have run out.

The Times described his award as being earned for 'services to journalism'. When the history of the post-war profession is written, one incident in his career will certainly be included. In 1978 he splashed across his front page a story concerning British Leyland. It alleged that the motor company had a 'slush fund' which it used to bribe its way into foreign markets. Fearlessly, the paper named names — Eric Varley, the Secretary of State for Industry; Don Ryder of the NEB; Alex Park, the Chief Executive. Of course, the whole farrago was pure invention. Fulsome retractions were published. Substantial damages were paid. The man who told the original lie went to prison. The man who fell for it and printed it in his newspaper has become a knight.

He may — at least for some time — be the last Fleet Street editor to do so. I could not find one of Sir David's rivals who would be prepared to accept an honour whilst in office. Some took a paradoxically aristocratic view — 'MBE for racing correspondents. That sort of thing is acceptable. But knighthoods for serving editors . . .!' Mike Molloy of the *Mirror* said if he were tapped on the shoulder many of his colleagues would think he was touched in the head.' Most of the people I like and respect would think the whole thing silly. And anyway,' he added, 'there are no free lunches.' Editors should not be in receipt of favours from party leaders.

I suspect that Mr Molloy might feel differently if the big buff envelope drops through his letter-box after he retires. Frank Giles of the *Sunday Times* and Charles Douglas-Home in charge of the Thunderer itself drew an absolute distinction between leaving presents and bonuses paid for satisfactory work.

Both insisted that they make no criticism of others who took a different view. Indeed, Mr Douglas-Home went so far as to say that 'any impropriety may be in the eye of the beholder' and Mr Giles was careful to speak of the 'implication' that the recipient was the 'Prime Minister's place man'. But they were all making the same point. Journalists cannot afford to accept favours from the people about whom they write.

In the past they have usually refused to do so. At the height of the *Mirror* group's infatuation with Harold Wilson, both

178

Hugh Cudlipp and Sydney Jacobson were offered knighthoods. Both believed that acceptance, whilst they were working on the paper, might at least appear to put them in the Prime Minister's pocket. So both declined with thanks.

William Connor's name appeared in an Honours List whilst he was still technically a *Mirror* columnist. But when the call came 'Cassandra' was dying. And in any case, William Connor did not determine the editorial policy of the *Mirror*. It is the men and women who decide whether or not to turn their papers into propaganda sheets who ought to refuse the Establishment's stifling embrace.

Let us think for a moment of the dangers which Sir David English now faces. During the last General Election he devoted an entire front page to a story which he boldly headed 'Twelve Labour Lies'. It turned out that most of the information below the headline had been taken from a Conservative Central office hand-out and after the new Government took office most of the 'lies' proved to be accurate predictions. But it was assumed that the then Mr English was guilty of nothing more serious than sloppy editing, that he did not ask about the story's origins and that he genuinely believed it to be true.

What will happen if, during the next General Election, Sir David appears to be acting in the interests of Mrs Thatcher and her party? If prejudiced observers call the *Daily Mail* no more than a Tory Party news-sheet, if his editorials seem biased and his news stories appear to be a product of prejudices rather than carefully researched information? It will be much more difficult for the defenders to claim that all the inadequacies are simply the result of incompetence — rather like the discovery of El Dorado in the Amazon jungle that he reported a couple of years ago. He has become the Prime Minister's man, and he will retain that liability.

Express Delivery

REGULAR READERS OF this column may well have noticed that I cannot fairly be described as an unequivocal admirer of the *Sun* and *Daily Express*. But 'fair do's', as they say where I come from. This week the column must contain a gracious admission and a grudging compliment. During the last ten days both of those papers have genuinely made, as well as reported, the news. Without the *Daily Express*, 'The Intruder at the Queen's Bedside' story might have leaked out drop by drop. But it would not have had the explosive impact of the sudden Monday morning revelation. Had it not been for the *Sun,* the sad tale of Commander Michael Trestrail might have remained behind the Buckingham Palace railings. Even the ranks of Tuscany — amongst whom, so far as those two papers are concerned, I number — could not quite forbear to cheer.

For the *Sun* my ovation is, admittedly, less than rapturous. There is, or there ought to be, something shameful about being the paper that a male prostitute approaches, when he wants to sell the story of his long-term liaison with a middle-aged policemen. But whatever the *Sun's* previous record, in the case of 'The Queen's Police Officer' they behaved with complete propriety. Payment was refused. Palace and police were informed. And whatever dangers the Queen endured from the continued proximity of Commander Trestrail was speedily removed. The Home Secretary was scrupulous in not revealing that the scandal had been unearthed by a newspaper. But the secret did not endure very long. Within twenty-four hours of the resignation, the *Sun* was taking the credit.

The *Daily Express,* on the other hand, never even affected reticence about the scoop, describing how the Queen 'kept him talking for ten minutes . . . then a footman came to her aid'. Once they were sure that the story was true there was no question of Palace warning or police tip-off, or a period of silence whilst the spikes were sharpened on the top of the Buck House walls. After all, the Queen already knew that a man had burst into her bedroom and sat on the edge of the royal bed. And it was reasonable to assume that as soon as the bad news reached Downing Street action was necessary.

In one particular at least, the 'astonishing story of how an intruder in Buckingham Palace sat for ten minutes on the Queen's bed' produced an immediate response. On the day that the scoop appeared in print the Prime Minister made a well-publicized trip down the Mall for an unscheduled audience with the Queen. According to her press office, Mrs Thatcher was anxious to express to the Queen her immediate apologies for the gross lapse in security. No doubt their version of events was correct. But the Prime Minister had known of the break-in since Friday. It was three days later that she prostrated herself before the Sovereign. Her response was certainly 'immediate'. She acted immediately the *Daily Express* ran the story.

Had the *Daily Express* not blown the gaff, the whole thing would, of course, have been hushed up. The people who still claim to be security advisers would have argued that once the ridiculous facts were known, regiments of copy-cat desperadoes would start to prowl Constitution Hill armed with grappling irons and scaling ladders. No one should blame them for giving that prudent advice. But equally no one should criticize the *Daily Express* for choosing to print the scoop of the year. There is a genuine public interest element in the exposure of such crass incompetence. We need not pretend that 'the voice of Britain' was reluctant to do its duty. But for once, a newspaper's duty and self-interest did not diverge.

If Norman Luck (the happily named third of the by-line on the sensational story) is to be believed, the *Daily Express* almost ignored the tip-off about the 'drama that began early in the morning in the Queen's first floor bedroom'. The whole anecdote seemed literally incredible and Luck initially feared that he was the victim of a not very sophisticated hoax. The *Sunday Mirror* was whispered the same news at about the same time and — had it believed the unbelievable — could have published the sensational story twenty-four hours before the *Express* exploded the bombshell. But the *Sunday Mirror* was still smarting from the Buckingham Palace denial of its 'Prince of Wales in Train Assignation' story. It decided on caution — and missed the scoop of the year.

The *Daily Express,* anxious not to become Fleet Street's fool, started checking — torn between the terror of publishing fantasy and the fear of alerting its rivals to what it hoped might be a world exclusive. Neither Buckingham Palace nor Scotland Yard had anything to say and Luck found their silence encouraging. So *Express* specialists were asked to tap their private reservoirs of information. Percy Hoskins, the retired crime reporter, pumped his police contacts. Political Editor John Warden spoke to civil servants who could be relied upon for private information as a demonstration of their importance. Both men reported the result of their enquiries to Ted Dickinson, the *Daily Express* deputy editor. Their conclusion was that the unbelievable was true.

Because of fears about the contempt laws, the story was published without revealing the intruder's name. But Fagan's anonymity lasted for only a few hours. The following day, the newspapers were packed with compromising trivia about the early morning intruder, the Attorney General issued a carefully worded warning and Mr Fagan senior sat in the corner of Islington's Grosvenor public house talking to whichever journalist filled his glass. Now the contracts have been signed and the various Fagan stories are the exclusive property of the papers which have bought them. In short, we are down again to the lowest common denominator. But the *Daily Express* sent the Prime Minister scurrying to the Palace last week, and that is an enviable achievement.

Guardian Angels

ON MONDAYS THE *Guardian* has Posy Simmonds and that is, in itself, sufficient reason for forking out 23p. Ms Simmonds draws the biggest and best strip cartoon in Fleet Street. Each week she covers seventy or eighty square inches at the bottom of what is called 'Guardian Women'. I have no doubt that one day her three-decker, ten-frame cartoons will be cut up and sold in priceless pieces like Manet's *Execution of Emperor Maximilian*. In the meantime, the drawings and their inseparable stories manage to be simultaneously endearing and astringent. The Posy cartoon is the sort of thing that gives charm a good name. The *Guardian* is lucky to have found her.

Ms Simmonds insists that *she* found the *Guardian,* as she touted her portfolio of freelance drawings from art editor to art editor and persuaded the people in Farringdon Road to commission the occasional sketch to 'fill a hole in the features page'. Illustrating the work of the *Guardian's* illustrious writers seemed to her a chance to comment on, as well as to clarify, the stories. The editor, Peter Preston, must have noticed her talent for drawing an opinion. For one day, in Ms Simmond's own words, 'We were in a lift and he asked me to do a strip.'

Were I to make a puerile joke related to the way in which Ms Simmonds described Mr Preston's request, I would qualify for a Monday morning place next to her in the *Guardian.* For caged in close proximity to the stories of the Weber family and their friends is the 'Naked Ape' — cuttings culled from other publications by the *Guardian's* liberated readers and sent to their natural newspaper home to illustrate what I am sure they call "institutional sexism".

There was a time when the space which Ms Simmonds now fills with such legal elegance itself might have at least qualified as a bald monkey. Varoomshka, the previous strip cartoon's eponymous heroine, was part Greek chorus and part Shakespeare fool. She was also a bare-breasted, white-thighed Amazon who passed through the world of the rich and famous, asking simple questions which revealed either the depth of their folly or the inevitability of their downfall. Despite being a young lady of exceptional physique, Varoomshka played the part of Every-woman.

Now, next to the awful puns ('We made only two boobs last year') and the venerable prejudices ('Edinburgh Kitchen Centre introduces better working conditions for women') Posy Simmonds draws Benji, a three-year-old who will never grow up because his father had a vasectomy in a previous episode and his creator needs a child of that age and innocence to draw silent attention to the foibles and follies of his elders if not betters. Ms Simmonds is commendably unpretentious about her characters. But if pressed she will admit it. Benji is Every-child.

The Simmonds ménage of socially aware polytechnic lecturers, unfaithful advertising executives, aggressive art students and harassed (dare I use the word?) housewives evolved out of a strange school story — 'The Silent Three of St Botolph's'. The teenage trio (who might have been created by Arthur Marshall) first grew up and then, crossed with the randy Teddy Bear that Ms Simmonds also created, turned into Weber and Co. It has always seemed to me that what they say about a woman's lot amongst the new uncertain middle classes is far more revealing than the quotations that appear in 'Naked Ape'. For the snippets from real life on the left of the page often seem risibly ridiculous. Whilst art, on the right, clearly imitates life.

I can, for instance, easily imagine Jocasta (the overweight student) or Wendy (the less than glamorous wife and mother) traipsing off to Covent Garden to find fitness and eternal youth in the Pineapple Dance Studios, an institution that has recently been much discussed in the business pages of the posh papers. Even those of us who are slightly sceptical about the very existence of the society which 'Naked Ape' seeks to expose, cannot have failed to be impressed by the special asset that helped the story of Pineapple into the news. The asset is the firm's boss, Debbie Moore. She was described under an *Observer* picture as 'the latest and most beautiful recruit to the ranks' of company chairmen. In the *Sunday Times* she wore shorts. The *Guardian* itself portrayed Ms Moore in a leotard which, in Frank Sinatra's immortal words, made her legs seem to reach up to her chin.

Of course, it was all legit. Stories about British Leyland's exports are accompanied by pictures of ten-ton lorries. And on the Sunday of Pineapple's emergence there were photographs (in the *Sunday Times*) of Roland Smith proving his determination to keep control of the Knightsbridge emporium by holding a Harrods carrier aloft and Paul Wolf (in the *Observer*) demonstrating his flair for fashion by pushing his training-shoe-encased feet in the direction of the camera. But if a male, such as Bernard Thomas, the diminutive genius who flexes the English cricketers' muscles, was to move his gymnasium from Birmingham to London, would the new company get the same coverage as Ms Moore — even in the *Guardian* where they try to be careful about such things.

That is a moral dilemma for Jill Tweedie and Polly Toynbee to resolve in a way which is consistent with 'Guardian

184

Women's' conscience — a dilemma which I hope they can overcome without causing the mayhem which would come from calling Kenneth Saunders (the offending photographer) a traitor to the *Guardian's* standards of sexual respect. I propose to make no complaint about the title of a neighbouring article — 'A hetero sissy's way with women'. It appeared on a Saturday; not a bad day in the *Guardian's* week. A trumpet of a prophecy. O wind, if 'Weekend Guardian' comes, can Posy Simmonds be far behind?

Royal Blues

AN ACQUAINTANCE OF mine who works for a tabloid daily has suddenly begun to suffer from insomnia. Each night the sleep of the just is disturbed by a recurrent nightmare. It all begins innocently enough with the arrival of his morning paper. But then the banner headline leaps at him from the front page. The construction and subject are always the same. Prince William Not To Join Cambridge Communist Club. Philip and Joan Collins Rumour Groundless. Queen Mum Never Met Ku Klux Klan Lookalike. Koo Stark Not Sighted in Knightsbridge Store.

My friend lies awake staring at the ceiling and trying to remember if those headlines have really been printed or if they are just the shape of enormities to come. Now that the *Star* has promised to back away from the Palace keyhole, he may have fewer sleepless nights. But reading the small print of their promise, I doubt it.

I do not believe that even my fervid friend ever dreamed that on the same Sunday two papers would claim to have psychoanalysed the Princess of Wales. Yet it happened. *The News of the World* published a 'psychiatrist's casebook' complete with a little simulation of half a page torn from the doctor's record — 'daughter of broken home . . . bouts of temper and independence'. Connoisseurs of Fleet Street noted with interest that in Rupert Murdoch's papers 'independence' is listed as a symptom of the sickness that ends with the patient's head being examined.

The *Mail on Sunday* actually named the psychiatrist

behind the long-range telescope. Dr Thomas Holmes's diagnosis was significantly less positive than the 'Diana Heading for a Breakdown' headline. Indeed, the 'astonishing warning' was something of an anticlimax. 'If she is not already sick,' Dr Thomas concluded, 'there is a real chance she may become ill.' For readers who felt that the same prognosis might be made about the whole female population, he edged slightly nearer to a medical opinion. 'An obsessive compulsive illness could definitely be a possibility,' he opined, basing his judgement on 'the known facts as published in the Press . . . set against the Holmes-Rahe Scale.'

You will of course recall that the *Mail on Sunday* is published for the respectable (and respectful) lower-middle classes. So in the interests of propriety it has to add a dismissive sentence that distances the paper from its own page three lead: 'Whether anyone will take this seriously or not is open to doubt, but Americans appear to.'

The note of militant chauvinism with which the disclaimer ends is in the great Rothermere tradition. And up the road in Bouverie Street the *News of the World* also stayed in character. 'All she needs is love,' warbled Unity Hall, matching spurious compassion and general prurience in equal measure.

It would be interesting to know what Dr Thomas Holmes and the *News of the World's* 'Top Harley Street psychiatrist' make of Fleet Street's obsession with the Royal Family in general and Princess Diana in particular. The Queen's opinion (expressed, I suspect, in more trenchant language than that used at the bedside by Dr Holmes) was made known to national editors when they were summoned to the Palace a year ago to be told that 'The Princess of Wales feels totally beleaguered.'

Since then intrusion has followed intrusion, described by an indignant *Sunday Telegraph* as 'sneak photographs of the Princess pregnant, fanciful tales of anorexia nervosa and even of marital break-up'. What a pity that Oliver Pritchett did not follow one of Sunday journalism's most hallowed traditions and 'name the guilty men'.

Most of them are, of course, employed by newspapers. But we would be wrong to excoriate them for the vulgarities of recent months without pleading in mitigation the circumstances which have (in that sanctimonious Victorian phrase) 'brought them so low'. Much of the responsibility must lie with the people not a million miles from Buckingham Palace — the people who encouraged the stories of the Sailor Prince and the Fairy Tale Princess. In the real world, it is not reasonable to rejoice at the publicity given to Prince Andrew's part in the Falklands Campaign and then deplore the coverage of his subsequent holiday arrangements. The picture of the returning warrior with the rose between his teeth was, metaphorically at least, taken by the same camera which tracked him through the Mustique undergrowth.

And I have no doubt that Princess Diana will continue to live the life of a goldfish in a constantly illuminated bowl.

'The Palace,' Oliver Pritchett told us in the *Sunday Telegraph,* is clearly delighted at the Princess's popularity and at the enormous public interest in her.' But, he went on to explain, the Court 'draws a line between legitimate interest in the public and official life of members of the Royal Family and their private life.' But the 'line is often blurred' and 'often it is Buckingham Palace itself that bends the rules.' Once upon a time in Ruritania the newspapers may have published only pictures in which the King wore a crown. But those days are over. Today, Black Michael would be paid a retainer by the *Sun.*

It would be impertinent for a loyal subject — and genuine admirer of the Royal Family — to offer advice about how the constant barrage of publicity should be faced. I therefore do no more than make a general judgement about the behaviour of the Press. It is a simple animal with simple tastes and a simple view about its duty to report what its customers want to read. If the newspaper-buying public is constantly told that 'News of the Royal Family is good for you' (and if, as is obviously the case in Britain, they enthusiastically believe it), the newspapers will feed them on Royal Family news at every meal — baked, boiled, fricasseed and if possible *au naturel.*

In short, the only way to lower the pressure on the Royal Family is to cool down the Press. And Fleet Street will steam on well above boiling point for as long as its customers remain obsessed by 'the Royals'.

After the Palace confrontation between Queen and Fourth Estate, one editor asked me a genuine (if rhetorical) question.

'What are they for,' he enquired, 'if it isn't to have their pictures taken?' Queen Victoria would not have been amused. But then she retired into obscurity for twenty years.

Envoi

AT NINE THIRTY-four next Friday morning (Prayers being over) Mr Frank Allaun will rise in his place on the Opposition benches of the House of Commons and move the Second Reading of the Right of Reply in the Media Bill. Mr Allaun knows my view of his proposals. His Bill is generally impracticable and wholly desirable, probably unworkable and certainly essential. Even if emasculated in Committee it would, once it matured from Bill to Law, cause our nastiest national daily newspapers constant embarrassment and inconvenience. It would also cost them money and circulation. I shall gladly vote for the Second Reading at half-past two next Friday afternoon.

So will a distinguished group of MPs. Indeed some of the supporters of Mr Allaun's Private Members Bill (Sir Derek Walker-Smith QC for example) have metamorphosed from distinguished Members of Parliament into distinguished Parliamentarians — a superior sort of legislative animal. The Right of Reply in the Media Bill is not a spasm of left-wing lunacy or a totalitarian plot to change the *Financial Times* into *Pravda*.

It simply proposes — admittedly in a slightly simplistic form — that 'members of the public, companies and organizations' should be given 'the right to reply to allegations made against them or to misreporting or misrepresentation concerning them in the Press or on radio or television'. And what could be fairer than that? After all, as the *Daily Mail,* the *Sun* and the *Daily Express* never cease to tell us, it is a free country. And in such a happy land, free men and women should enjoy the right to defend themselves against smears and slanders and to clear from their names the taint of false allegation — even if they are not Sir James Goldsmith and cannot afford £10,000 for legal fees.

I suspect that there will be considerable, if reluctant, public support for Mr Allaun's little Bill. For the British public is highly ambivalent about its newspaper and television. It enjoys a prurient glance behind Britt Ekland's curtains. But it wants to believe that Britt enjoys the notoriety. It likes to hear Roger Cook humiliating a rogue car dealer in his *Checkpoint* programme. But it needs the comforting certainty that the salesman is being persecuted on behalf of some impoverished innocent who has been exploited by the villain's cunning. It likes to be titillated by stories of vice and perversion. But it wants its conscience cleared by the eventual punishment of the wrongdoers. Newspapers are supposed to expose corruption, not enjoy it.

Above all, newspapers are supposed to be 'fair' and 'honest'. And support for Mr Allaun's Bill will be considerably increased by the mass of recent evidence to support the view that many of the national dailies do not even attempt to live up to their romantic reputations. Indeed, during the last fortnight three national dailies and two Sundays were adjudged by the Press Council to have behaved in a way which undermined most of the claims about honesty and fair play. All the papers were in pursuit of stories concerning Peter Sutcliffe — 'The Yorkshire Ripper'. The behaviour of one of them — the *Daily Mail* — would be beyond belief were it not for that paper's record, from the Zinoviev letter to the British Leyland slush fund. Dubious practices are to the *Mail* as typographical errors are to the *Guardian*.

Sir David English (the *Mail's* editor and a recent addition to the ranks of chivalry) told the Press Council that he had actually gone to the expense of an international telephone call in order to tell his deputy *not* to buy Mrs Sutcliffe's story. Indeed he believed that admirers of Lynda Lee-Potter's pulchritude, Paul Johnson's patriotism and Andrew Alexander's slightly punk Poujadism would be deeply offended if their paper paid money to a murderer's wife. So Mrs Sutcliffe was simply encouraged to believe (or deceived into believing, as some crude commentators might say) that the *Mail* might pay up.

The fact that money was mentioned to the unfortunate lady was not revealed to the Press Council by the *Mail* itself, but by Mrs Sutcliffe's solicitor. In the blustering leader in which the verray parfit gentil knight set out to justify his paper's conduct, Sir David explained that 'We did keep our lines of communication open in order to glean what background information we could from Sutcliffe's wife.' He then went on to ask, 'Does this subterfuge merit condemnation in the terms meted out to us by the Press Council?' — thus condemning himself by even considering that the question was reasonable.

The connection between the Press Council's condemnation of the *Mail* and Frank Allaun's Right of Reply in the Media Bill is more than just the increasing disquiet about the conduct of some newspapers. Both the speech which Mr Allaun made when trying to introduce a similar Bill last year and the conclusions of the Press Council reflect a growing conviction that if our least reputable newspapers will not regulate their own conduct, some statutory body will have to do it for them. Press Council Chairman, Patrick Neill QC, was explicit about the new code he had laid down to govern the potential purchase of the sordid stories sold by murderers and the witnesses at their trials. 'I expect the rule to be observed. If it is not, I think that people will start looking for another body, a statutory one, to replace the Press Council.'

If that statutory body is set up, it will do more than simply set out the terms on which murky memoirs can be bought. It will — inevitably — prevent intrusion into private lives, prohibit the invention of interviews and the fabrication of eyewitness accounts and (as Mr Allaun specifically proposes) it will oblige an editor to give equal space and prominence to the correction of 'a factually inaccurate or distorted report' within three days of the offending article's appearance. Such an Act of Parliament will be riddled with doubt and difficulty. Who decides on a story's accuracy? How is distortion defined?

In short, the introduction of statutory control *might* be a disaster for the papers who really do believe in fair play and freedom and do not (unlike the *Mail*) actually try to nobble other papers' stories by pretending to offer money for information they do not intend to buy. But if statutory controls do come about, do not blame Mr Frank Allaun and me. Blame the people whose behaviour has provoked the justified concern and the contempt.

Dates of Publication

Down Argentina Way

By Jingo!   14 April 1982
Picture Search   16 June 1982
Paper Tigers   19 May 1982
Articles of War   8 September 1982
Foreign Matter   19 January 1983
Less Than Franks   26 January 1983
Springing a Leak   2 February 1983

Once a Week

My Funny Valentine   10 February 1982
Spectator Sport   17 February 1982
Sermons of the Mount   5 May 1982
Avid Listener   18 August 1982
City Slickers   15 September 1982
King and Country   28 April 1982
Altered Statesman   30 June 1982

Nine Tenths of the Law

Eyes Down   4 November 1981
Tiny Hands   6 January 1982
Managing Editors   3 February 1982
Tough Times   3 March 1982
Rupert Bare   24 March 1982
Sinking Feeling   21 July 1982
Three Legs Bad   12 January 1983

Private Grief

Mother of Invention   24 February 1982
Street Price   24 November 1982
Last Exits   10 March 1982
A Touch of the Sun   4 August 1982
Cardinal Sin   8 December 1982
Gang Show   25 August 1982
Hard Pressed   5 January 1983

Within the Fringe

Spark Plugs   18 November 1981
Sinking Star   25 November 1981
Vox Pulp   11 August 1982
Pride and Prejudice   1 September 1982
Rural Reads   20 October 1982
Sporting Type   27 October 1982
Book Ends   23 February 1983

Only on Sundays

Bloody Sunday   23 September 1981
Vox Pop   21 October1981
Telegraph Lines   23/30 1981
All Human Life?   9 December 1981
Jameson Raid   13 January 1982
Death Wish   31 March 1982
Mail Disorder   26 May 1982

Lobby Terms

Rogues' Gallery   30 September 1981
Unbalancing the Budget   17 March 1982
Centre Court   14 July 1982
Printer's Devil   31 July 1982, *Guardian*
Labour Pains   6 October 1982
Nott Answering   13 October 1982
By-lines   3 November 1982

Court and Social

Engaging?   21 April 1982
Baby Bio   12 May 1982
Baby Talk   7 July 1982
Knight Editor   23 June 1982
Express Delivery   28 July 1982
Guardian Angels   10 November 1982
Royal Blues   9 February 1983
Envoi   16 February 1983